LEGGING IT

*Life Lessons Learned Thru-Hiking
the Appalachian Trail*

BY CRAIG CLAPPER AKA HOOSIER

Copyright © 2014 by Craig Clapper AKA Hoosier

Legging It
Life Lessons Learned Thru-Hiking the Appalachian Trail
by Craig Clapper AKA Hoosier

Printed in the United States of America

ISBN 9781498418850

All rights reserved solely by the author. The author guarantees all contents are original and do not infringe upon the legal rights of any other person or work. No part of this book may be reproduced in any form without the permission of the author. The views expressed in this book are not necessarily those of the publisher.

Scripture quotations taken from the English Standard Version (ESV). Copyright © 2001 by Crossway, a publishing ministry of Good News Publishers. Used by permission. All rights reserved.

Scripture quotations taken from the New International Version (NIV). Copyright © 1973, 1978, 1984, 2011 by Biblica, Inc.™. Used by permission. All rights reserved.

Scripture quotations taken from the King James Version (KJV) – *public domain*

Scripture quotations taken from The Message (MSG). Copyright © 1993, 1994, 1995, 1996, 2000, 2001, 2002. Used by permission of NavPress Publishing Group. Used by permission. All rights reserved.

Scripture quotations taken from the New American Standard Bible (NASB). Copyright © 1960, 1962, 1963, 1968, 1971, 1972, 1973, 1975, 1977, 1995 by The Lockman Foundation. Used by permission. All rights reserved.

Scripture quotations taken from the New English Translation (NET Bible). Copyright ©1996-2006 by Biblical Studies Press, L.L.C. Used by permission. All rights reserved.

Scripture quotations taken from the American Standard Version (ASV) – *public domain*

Scripture quotations taken from the New Living Translation (NLT). Copyright © 1996, 2004, 2007 by Tyndale House Foundation. Used by permission. All rights reserved.

www.xulonpress.com

Dedicated to fellow pilgrims:
"Blessed are those whose strength is in you,
whose hearts are set on pilgrimage."
– Psalm 84:5 (NIV)

The Appalachian Trail is a physical, mental, and spiritual journey. In *Legging It*, Craig Clapper weaves the story of the trail into his faith journey. He provides practical take-aways to encourage and help Christians on the path of Life.
Jennifer Pharr Davis
Hiker, Author, Speaker. www.blueridgehikingco.com

Meeting Hoosier on Mount Katahdin in 2007 helped me prepare and deal with the difficulties the trail of life has brought my way as a teacher in Newtown, Connecticut. *Legging It* will help you prepare for whatever you may face in life.
Kristin Violette
Newtown School Teacher/ Outdoor Enthusiast

Hoosier loves God and genuinely loved and cared about those he met on the trail. Hikers sensed this and were drawn to him. I am sure you will sense the same thing on each page of this book.
Bruce Sparks, AKA Sparks
District Executive, Michigan Crossroads Council, Boy Scouts of America

In *Legging It* the reader will be taken on three journeys simultaneously. The obvious is the physical hike itself and the sights, sounds, pain, and misery a hiker will undergo on a thru-hike of the 2,186 mile Appalachian Trail. The second journey is a journey in mind and spirit. Who you really are and what you were intended to be will need to be resolved as you journey in solitude. The third journey, the spiritual journey, is what sets *Legging It* apart from most hiking books. The scripture verses "Hoosier" applies to his hike, taken from the best guide book ever written, can guide you on your own journey in life.
Paul Stutzman
Author of *Hiking Through*, *Biking Across America*, and several Amish novels. www.paulstutzman.com

Before beginning my 2013 thru-hike, I prayed God would bring Christian men into my life. Hoosier was an answer to that prayer. He was a very compatible hiking partner, spiritual inspiration, and has become a close friend. This book contains the stories of the many lives like mine he touched along the trail.
Bill Wasser, AKA Samson
Professional Skydiver/ 2013 Thru-hiker

I don't remember every shelter I slept in or every mountain I climbed. What I remember is the lifelong friendships I acquired along the way.

Hoosier was not only a hiking buddy but also a great friend. His spiritual guidance is one of the many reasons I made it to Maine.
Josh "Rash" Calhoun
Founder of The Sportsman's Wish Foundation

TABLE OF CONTENTS

Introduction xi

The Beginning and First Steps............................. 21
Traveling Light: Getting Rid of Weight 24
Traveling Tight: Traveling with Friends...................... 28
Traveling Right: Following the White Blazes 46
Trail Blight: Challenges Along the Way...................... 51
Spiritual Might: Longing for the Spiritual Connections 60
Angels in Flight—Trail Magic: People Who Share at
Just the Right Time 76
Traveling With Delight: Enjoying the Journey 86
Traveling With the End in Sight: Staying Committed
Despite the Difficulty 95
The Joy of Completion: Tetelestai! It Is Finished! 103

Pastor David Burnham often referred to John Bunyan's classic *The Pilgrim's Progress* in his sermons. The description of the Christian life as a spiritual pilgrimage resonated deeply within me and inspired me to see my thru-hike of the Appalachian Trail as one as well. Thank you, David.

Jenny Heiter was my editor. Her encouragement and belief in the book kept me at the task when I wanted to quit, and her love of words and editing skills made my writings publishable. Thank you, Jenny.

The most-asked question about my hike has been, "What did your wife think about your being gone so long?" I answer, "I married the right woman. Jan understood my desire to become a thru-hiker, fully supported the venture, and rejoiced with me when I reached Katahdin." Thank you, Jan. I love you.

David and Mary O'Brien were exceptional Trail Angels to Sparks and me. Thank you, O'Briens.

INTRODUCTION

I took my first step on the Appalachian Trail with the intent of hiking the entire 2,186 miles and thus obtaining the title "thru-hiker." This desire was birthed nearly twenty years earlier when I read an article about the trail and those who complete it within one calendar year: people called thru-hikers. I remember thinking that one day I had to do that. I actually felt there was a divine call upon my life to do so.

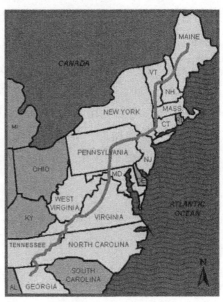

The Appalachian Trail

That desire led to years of section hiking the trail a week or two at a time and spending nearly two months on the trail in 2007. Those hikes only deepened my desire to one day become a thru-hiker. The 2007 hike covered the final and most difficult states of the trail: Vermont, New Hampshire, and Maine.

Accomplishing that hike gave me confidence that I could complete a thru-hike.

I also met thru-hikers who were nearing completion of the trail and grew to admire them for the character traits it took for them to get that far.

Being from Indiana, I had taken the trail name Hoosier nearly twenty years earlier, and Bruce Sparks, a friend who would be joining me for the first two months, took the trail name Sparks from his last name. We knew statistically that only around twenty percent of those who begin the journey complete it. I wanted to join their ranks. Could I accomplish such a monumental task? I would soon find out. I could only guess at how challenging the next five to six months would be. For now, I needed to take the second of approximately five million steps to the northern terminus of the Appalachian Trail, Mount Katahdin.

FIRST STEPS

Hoosier and Sparks

S pringer Mountain, Georgia, the southern terminus of the Appalachian Trail, is not easy to get to. Most thru-hikers hike the nearly nine-mile approach trail from Amacalola Falls State Park in order to reach the plaque indicating the beginning of the AT. Sparks and I hiked the nine-mile approach trail.

It was spitting snow as we started toward Springer Mountain when a park ranger greeted us and warned us that the weather forecast was calling for a couple inches of snow and temperatures in the teens. We assured him that we were prepared for such weather since we lived up north and were used to snow and cold temperatures. A few miles later, we met a hiker going south. She said she had spent the night on Springer Mountain and was going to return to the park lodge to wait out the bad weather before continuing her thru-hike. Sparks and I later commented to each other that she was going to be waiting a long time. We didn't expect to see her again, and we didn't. Little did we know that the month of March would prove to be the snowiest and coldest for Georgia and North Carolina in years, and many would-be thru-hikers would get "off trail."

When we arrived at the long-anticipated plaque that announced the southern terminus of the AT, we were greeted by high winds, snow, and such cold temperatures that we stayed only a few minutes. It was a practical rather than a memorable beginning to the long journey.

On Springer Mountain we met another hiker with the trail name Shepherd. He and I had been reading one another's online trail journals in the months preceding the hike, so it seemed almost like a reunion. Shepherd had taken his trail name from his title as a leader in his church youth group. I knew from his journal entries that Shepherd hiked in a kilt and would be getting off trail often to go to folk dances.

He was very different from me and Sparks, but I liked the difference. I grew to love this aspect of the hike: thru-hikers are a very diverse group of people with a common path and goal, which would bind us together in a deep way. But for now it was bitter cold, and we needed to get moving. So we took a few pictures and passed our first blaze, or trail marker, of the Appalachian Trail.

Momma Bear in Trouble

Our first day into the hike, we came across a homeschooling mother, her three young children, and their dog. They were from Florida and were not prepared for the weather we were experiencing. That evening Sparks and I watched as she set up camp and made dinner for her family. She was quite knowledgeable and one tough lady. I gave her the trail name Supermom but found out later she already had been given the trail name Momma Bear by other hikers. What she was attempting was admirable: the children had wonderful attitudes and were not complaining, but they were in trouble. The children huddled around the campfire that evening with other hikers trying to dry out their cotton socks and wet gloves but to no avail. Various hikers helped out, but it was evident that they were in over their heads. We later learned that they went back to Florida a few days later. She represented many of the hikers we would meet in the first few weeks of the hike who began the journey with great intentions but were naïve to what the trail could throw at them. Others we came across had forty-degree sleeping bags, cotton clothes, and way too much weight both on their bodies and in their packs.

Twenty Percent

The first real chance to obtain the right gear, get rid of unneeded gear, or get off the trail was two days ahead at Neels

Gap. Statistics show that nearly twenty percent of would-be thru-hikers get off there.

Our third day in, the skies cleared, and although still cold, we had great views of the mountains and valleys surrounding us. The recently fallen snow gave everything a clean, crisp feel and look, and with no leaves on the trees, I could see for miles. Sparks and I stopped at Blood Mountain to take in the view along with five thru-hikers who were sunning themselves on a giant rock slab. I asked a few questions and found that they had met on the trail and had decided to hike together. I also asked if I could take a picture of them, and they heartily agreed to do so and posed. After taking the picture, I shared with them that I did not want to discourage anyone but that I wanted the picture of the five of them to later share that statistically only one of these five hikers would make it to Katahdin. They didn't seem to be discouraged but rather humored by my statement. I am sure they, like me, could not imagine not finishing. Still, I assume they, also like me, knew deep inside that it could happen. The statistics are sobering.

We expected the unseasonably cold weather to pass.

It didn't.

Chow

People often ask how hikers obtain food while hiking the AT. Hikers obviously cannot carry enough food for the entire journey, which is where "trail towns" come in. Trail towns are usually very small towns within "hitching distance" of the AT: usually four to five hiking days' distance from one another. Locals are mostly enthusiastic about picking up hikers and taking them to town. Once in town, hikers first seek out the closest all-you-can-eat buffet and eat and eat and eat a little more. Then hikers search for a hostel or hiker-friendly motel. A shower and laundry is next priority before finding the local grocery store to resupply for another four to five days on the trail. Excitement fills conversations on the trail as hikers get within a day or two of the next trail town. Shelter journals or south bounders are where we share information as to the best place to stay, where to eat, and who the Trail Angels are in the town.

Two days before reaching Erwin, Tennessee, I came upon a group of guys excitedly talking about what they were looking forward to in Erwin. It was the AYCE Kentucky Fried Chicken Buffet. I remember thinking, they are going to lose money off that bunch!

Food is perhaps the dominant topic of conversation on the trail. However, another dominant topic of conversation the couple days before reaching Erwin was church, since we would be arriving in Erwin Easter weekend. Many hikers were putting in "big miles" in order to arrive in time to attend Easter Sunday services. This actually startled me because I was living with many of these hikers and would not describe them as religious. I thought about this while hiking and remembered Jesus' quote from Deuteronomy 8 when He was hungry and tempted by Satan in the wilderness to turn stones into bread. "Jesus answered, 'It is written: man shall not live by bread alone but on every word that comes from the mouth of God.'" Could it be that these hikers were reflecting the fact that they were not only physical beings longing to feed their bodies but also spiritual beings longing to feed their souls? Perhaps living in the beauty of God's creation and having extended time to think deeply had awakened a spiritual hunger, a desire to know and worship God their creator.

Typical Thru-Hikers

Although thru-hikers come from various countries, walks of life, and age groups, there are two "typical" thru-hikers.

The first are recent college graduates in their early twenties who find it difficult to find a job after graduation. So, they take a hike. Or perhaps they can get a job but decide it is now or never to accomplish this dream of becoming a thru-hiker. They are usually healthy, smart, independent, and adventurous. They are strong hikers who enjoy making friends on the trail but are often low on finances and have to live frugally on the trail. Toward the end of the hike, some are dependent upon trail magic and hiker boxes to make it to Katahdin. They also tend to be under a time constraint and need to put in big miles to finish on time. If they do not complete the trail, it is often due to injuries incurred by pushing too hard. If this group of hikers were trying to find an answer to life on the trail, it would be, "What am I going to do with my life, and where do I fit in?"

One such hiker who earned the trail name Heavyweight was carrying outdated heavy gear. I heard that someone told him he ought to update his gear. He replied, "I would if someone would buy it for me!" He was a strong hiker and did complete the hike even with his outdated, heavy gear.

The second group are predominantly men, but still some women, in their fifties or early sixties. These hikers are usually going through a major transition in life. Many have recently retired, some in order to hike the trail. Others have lost their jobs or a mate through death or divorce. They, too, are asking certain questions about life that they hope to find answers to on the trail. Their questions tend to be, "What am I going to do with the rest of my life? What changes do I want to make for this final chapter of life? What legacy do I want to leave?"

I found both groups very open to discussing these life issues with me and believe the anonymity of the trail contributed to the openness. If hikers discovered I was a recently retired minister, they were usually even more willing to discuss deep issues with me.

No one knows the others' real names, only their trail name. I discovered from my earlier hikes that unless one of us made the effort after the trail, I would never see the person again.

Although most people are dealing with these issues, very few are able to take a considerable length of undistracted time to think deeply about them. Many thru-hikers shared with me that they were not religious but were spiritual and hoped that the hike would be a spiritual journey for them as well.

I found the trail to be a wonderful "church": we had a beautiful sanctuary, a cathedral of green to worship in. I think green might be God's favorite color. I also found a "congregation" of people who were very interested in thinking deeply about life, God, and what kind of person they want to be.

Perhaps we could learn something from Jesus who spent most of His time hiking throughout Galilee with a group of spiritually open followers around the Sea of Galilee, preaching along its shores, fields, and rural villages.

A Little Foreshadowing

I began this amazing journey on March 2nd at Springer Mountain, Georgia, and summited Mount Katahdin on September 21st. I can truthfully say that God walked with me the entire journey, and it is by His grace that I am now a thru-hiker. Since returning home, every day I think of the trail, all the fellow hikers I met, and the lessons I learned on the trail. I pray the following musings will inspire and instruct you in your journey through life. May you be a spiritual thru-hiker for God as you follow Jesus on the trail He has laid out for you.

One final note before proceeding with the book: Unless noted, the unmarked Scripture version I use is the ESV. While the KJV uses "conversation" and the NIV uses "life" or "live," I appreciate the ESV's use of "walk" to depict our journey on this planet.

TRAVEL FORESIGHT: THE BEGINNING AND FIRST STEPS

Looking Back and Looking Forward

The life of Jesus from age twelve through thirty is summed up in Luke 2:52 where Luke states that Jesus "grew in wisdom, stature, and in favor with God and men."

At the end of each year, I review the past year to determine if I have grown in the following four areas, and I set goals for the next year; that year, these goals included the thru-hike.

Wisdom: I constantly read all I could about the trail and gear. I corresponded with those who had accomplished the task. I wanted to be as knowledgeable as possible, and I was not too proud to ask for help.

Stature: I worked hard at being physically fit. Before beginning, I hiked six-thousand footers and swam in Wyoming where I visited my son for a couple months. Although I didn't really have weight to lose, I was trying to eat healthily. Two months before I started, I began hiking with a pack on and increased the weight each week.

Favor with God: I was hoping to be in such a healthy relationship with God that I was a living example of Jesus on the trail.

I needed to know well the One I hoped to share about. Since I was not currently preparing sermons each week, it was enlightening and freeing to read large portions of Scripture each day with myself in mind rather than the guy in the pew. I also studied in depth the book of Ephesians, which continually refers to the Christian life as a walk. I believe that a walk is the most-used metaphor in Scripture for the Christian life.

Favor with Man: From past section hikes on the Trail, I can say that some of the most giving, funny, eccentric, and interesting people I ever met I met on the trail. I looked forward to getting to know many thru-hikers on this adventure.

These were my goals. I started on them right away.

The Right Clothes

Someone said, "There is no such thing as bad weather, just bad clothing."

During my preparation hikes, I experienced just about every type of weather that could be thrown at me. I learned to enjoy and appreciate them all, which was primarily due to being prepared by wearing the right clothing.

I was sure the same would hold true mentally and emotionally as well while I hiked the AT. My preparation would determine if I would be able to enjoy and appreciate the hike rather than just endure the difficulties that would surely confront me. The spiritual preparation that comes from a rich relationship with God is the preparation we most need.

A Footnote

At eighty-five years old, my mother received her first pedicure. Her statement afterward was, "Why did I wait so long?" We tend to neglect our feet—but they are extremely important.

Our feet took a beating on the Appalachian Trail. At periodic breaks, hikers aired out their boots, socks, and feet. Most hikers, including me, had black toenails from the constant rubbing against the toe of our boots. In Tennessee one hiker looked at my feet and said, "Hoosier, why don't you just put a tag on it?" since my feet looked like they belonged to a dead man.

Scripture has a lot to say about feet; for instance, Isaiah 52:7 says, "How beautiful upon the mountains are the feet of him that bringeth good tidings, that publisheth peace; that bringeth good tidings of good, that publisheth salvation; that saith unto Zion, Thy God reigneth!" (KJV). Our feet are to take us to others to share a message from God. Ephesians 6:15 says "having shod your feet with the preparation of the gospel of peace" (NASB). Not only was I working to keep my physical feet in shape on the trail but also hoping they were the vehicle to share the good news of God's offer of peace through Jesus Christ.

TRAVELING LIGHT: GETTING RID OF WEIGHT

Gear Shift

Neels Gap plus the approach trail, around forty miles into the Appalachian Trail, is where approximately twenty percent of thru-hikers get off the trail and go home. I used to wonder how they could give up on the journey so soon. Now I understood. The hike had not been easy. At that point hikers were usually carrying extra weight in their packs and on their bodies.

Employees, legends such as Baltimore Jack, Pirate, and Lumpy, who have successfully completed the trail, offer a free "shake down" at an outfitter store at Neels Gap. All thru-hikers are striving to get their packs as light as possible for the upcoming hike. Each year Mountain Crossings Outfitters sends home approximately four-and-a-half tons of gear. I know a person who actually removed several feet of unneeded dental floss in order to eliminate excess weight. Guns, axes, machetes, hatchets, and large knives are just a few of the items that are often sent home. It really isn't that dangerous on the AT, but what is dangerous is carrying too much weight and jeopardizing the hike. Hikers who continue usually do so with several pounds less in their packs. If they continue, their bodies will shed several pounds as well.

Spiritually speaking, I believe we could all use a "shake down" to help us continue and complete the trail of life God has called us to. Hebrews 12:1 states that we ought to throw off any weight that would slow us down in our spiritual journey. I desire to travel light in my spiritual pilgrimage as well. I wonder what extra baggage I am carrying through life? I prayed that the extended time in the woods would give me a clear picture of just who I was and how I was traveling through life off trail. I hoped that this hike would be a life-changing event. I wondered what needed to go and what was really needed.

Packing Weariness

Sparks and I arrived cold and weary to Hot Springs, North Carolina, one of my favorite trail towns. The weather report called for even colder temperatures and snow for the next day. Most of the hikers in Hot Springs were planning to take a zero, a day off, due to the weather. However, Sparks, Nickelodian, and I decided to take Chuck Norris, who runs the Laughing Heart Hostel, up on an offer to "slack-pack" us: carrying just the necessities of the day, including our tents and sleeping bags, in case we got stuck in the storm since carrying fifteen pounds is so much easier than the usual thirty-five. So early the next morning, Chuck drove us fifteen miles north to Allen Gap. We then hiked back through the beautiful snow to enjoy another night in Hot Springs. The following morning Chuck drove us back with full packs to Allen Gap to continue our journey north.

I was really enjoying the hike and was singing the song "Walking in a Winter Wonderland." We passed a northbound section hiker with a very heavy pack. Referring to the beautiful falling snow, I said, "Beautiful day, isn't it!"

"I hadn't noticed," he grunted without even looking up as he passed by.

The exchange reminded me of how important it is to travel light, on and off trail. In a sense we should always be slack packing. Peter was a slack packer. In 1 Peter 5 he writes, "Cast all your cares upon Him because He cares for you" (NET). He was referring to Jesus whom he had heard say in Matthew 11:28, "Come to Me, all you who are weary and heavy-laden, and I will give you rest" (NASB).

Sometimes we too are called upon to slack-pack others in life. In Galatians 6:2 Paul says, "Bear one another's burdens, and so fulfill the law of Christ."

There are many kinds of burdens people are carrying in life. For some on the trail, it was the burden of limited finances. Just before coming into Hot Springs, Sparks and I came across a hiker who because of financial issues was going to camp in the cold. Instead, we put him up for the night at Laughing Heart Hostel. Doing so brought joy to our hearts and fulfilled the law of Christ, which is love. Pretty good deal for $15!

Barbed Wire

In Grayson Highlands I somehow got into some barbed wire and cut my leg up pretty badly; my leg was not doing well. I considered taking a zero. However, I would have lost my group, or "bubble," and it would have set Sparks back because he would have stayed with me. We were trying to get Sparks one hundred miles to McAffee Knob, a beautiful overlook one-third of the way through the AT and one of the most photographed spots on the Appalachian Trail. He had only a few days left to hike before he needed to return home.

As it turned out, Mot's wife Paula visited Mot and carried the majority of our gear by car twenty miles ahead. By carrying a light load, I was able to hike. Then we arranged to have the majority of our gear transported again so that I could stay on the trail. Sparks was carrying my gear, thus fulfilling what is called "the law of Christ."

It was a very difficult day for me physically. I just set my face to the grind and put in a long, hard day. Life is like that at times, and it was even for Jesus. The Gospel of Luke 9:51 states that "When the days drew near for him to be taken up, he **set his face** to go to Jerusalem" [emphasis added].

TRAVELING TIGHT: TRAVELING WITH FRIENDS

Being With and Without

In 2007 I hiked the states of Vermont, New Hampshire, and Maine while on a sabbatical. For the first five hundred of those six hundred miles, I hiked alone, that is, without human companionship, but God was my constant and very real companion. Being alone gives uninterrupted time for reflection and prayer, and I have found that I need time alone so that when I am with people, I am worth being with and have something to offer.

I believe that was the journey I was meant to be on at that time, but my thru-hike was different. The first seven weeks I had the companionship of my good friend Bruce Sparks. Throughout the journey I had the privilege of hiking with Samson, Joe the Hiker, Caribou, Dovetail, Rash, Mot, Punkin Pie, Nickelodian, Z, Breitside, Hobbit, Gummy Bear, Snowfrog, Bean, and others. I loved the companionship.

All this reminds me of the journeys of the Apostle Paul. He is constantly sharing whom he is with, where other companions are, and how their missionary journeys are going. He longs to see them, and they long to see him. The Christian life is a life lived in relationship with God; however, we are brought into a community with others who are on the same journey as followers of Jesus.

There are tremendous benefits to hiking with companions. Ecclesiastes 4:9-12 states, "Two are better than one, because they have a good return for their labor. If either of them falls down, one can help the other up. But pity anyone who falls and has no one to help them up. Also, if two lie down together, they will keep warm. But how can one keep warm alone? Though one may be overpowered, two can defend themselves. A cord of three strands is not quickly broken" (NIV).

Hiking alone and with a friend has different purposes and benefits. Jesus was a man of the people, a social being, and He spent countless hours with the disciples and other people. However, we also see Him often going off alone to pray. We need time alone with God, but we are also called to a journey with fellow pilgrims who are on the same path.

The Four Ls

While hiking, I thought of four things that were occurring on the trail.

First of all, I needed LEGS and LUNGS for the journey. There were LESSONS to be learned that related to life that I hoped to share when I got off the trail. But also there were LIVES. Other trails, such as the Pacific Crest and the Continental Divide, are less communal than the AT, I am told. The community of hikers became what I loved most about the trail.

That was a lesson for life as well; as the thru-hiker GRRRR said, "If it were just trails and trees, I would be off this thing, but it is the hiking community that keeps me on it," which is a great lesson for life off trail. It is the people in life who make the journey worth living.

Brief Encounters

I had a professor once say, "Never underestimate the power of a brief encounter." He then proceeded to give examples from Scripture where Jesus had brief encounters with people that proved to have profound implications. Nicodemus, Legion, the woman at the well, and several people He healed as He "passed by" are just a few.

In 2007, several years before my thru-hike, I hiked the states of Vermont, New Hampshire, and Maine. On the last night before completing the hike, several other hikers and I talked around a campfire. A young woman was there and was interested in some of the things I shared concerning spiritual issues. We exchanged email addresses and later became Facebook friends.

Six years later, Kristin and her boyfriend picked me up near the trail, fed me supper, did my laundry, gave me her car for the day, and even made arrangements for me to get a massage from one of her friends. They took me back to Kent, Connecticut, where I returned to the trail refreshed—all due to a "brief encounter." Every encounter we have is important and can have profound implications.

Never underestimate the power of a brief encounter.

God's Very First Thru-Hiker

Genesis 5 is a genealogy listing people who were born, had children, and then died. Boring! However, suddenly in the midst of the repetitive theme, one man stands out. Verse 22 reads, "Enoch walked with God **after** he fathered Methuselah . . ." [emphasis added]. Something about having a son had a profound impact upon Enoch. He started living differently. He now WALKED with God.

My favorite part of life on the trail was getting to know several other thru-hikers and their life stories. I often tell people off trail that no one takes several months out of life and hikes over two thousand miles who isn't working through something. Perhaps it was due to my having been a pastor or the anonymity of trail life (no one knows hikers' real names) that caused many hikers to share very personal life stories with me. Events had occurred in their lives that profoundly changed their futures. Most of these stories were tragic. They were on the trail to get some answers and new direction.

Several told me that they were actually grateful for what happened because it was what caused them to begin walking with God. I wish we were all smart enough to walk with God without something major coming into our lives to get our attention. For Enoch it was the blessing of the birth of a child. Too often though it is a life-shattering event. The good news is that God can take even these horrible experiences of life and bring good out of them.

SoBos

Righteous was my first SoBo: SoBos are southbounders. I was a NoBo, northbounder. There are usually only around two hundred SoBos who begin the AT in Maine in early June with the intent of finishing at Springer Mountain in September or October. SoBos encounter the most difficult terrain at the beginning of their hike. It was great to stop a few moments and share information and stories of what lay ahead for each of us: information such as where to find a good deli or ice cream, which hostels to stay in, and which to avoid. Trail conditions were also a common topic, with the answer usually being "lots of mud." We knew we would not see each other again, yet there was a unique connection since we were on the same path, going through the same difficulties, and experiencing the same joys. They admired us since we had hundreds of miles behind us, and we admired them since they went through the toughest five hundred miles the trail has to offer.

In Port Clinton, Pennsylvania, I took a zero to deal with blisters, buy new boots and hiking poles, resupply, and rest. At the hotel breakfast that morning, Smooth Sailin' showed up along with three thru-hikers I had never met: Olde English (from England), Chippy (from Brazil), and Eleven (from DC). We all shared trail stories. Olde English, Chippy, and I had an interesting conversation about how hikers seemed to get along so well and cared so much for each other even with such extremes differences. We discussed that although we were so diverse, whether NoBos or SoBos, we all shared a common and undisputed goal and path to get to our destination.

What if that were true of life off trail at our places of employment, in government, and most of all in the church?

Happy Hikers

Caribou and Dovetail, recent high-school graduates and best friends, were the happiest hikers I met on the trail. Their smiles and enthusiastic attitudes were contagious. I loved being around them. What amazed me was they loved being around Sparks and

Caribou and Dovetail

me and other older hikers. They would hike quickly during the day but end early, so we would catch them at a campsite that evening or as they took breaks whenever they came to a scenic overlook. They reminded me of Tom Sawyer and Huckleberry Finn on a great adventure. Caribou and Dovetail lived out King Solomon's advice recorded in Ecclesiastes 11:9: "You who are young, be happy while you are young, and let your heart give you joy in the days of your youth. Follow the ways of your heart and whatever your eyes see" (NIV).

These two friends were having the time of their lives. I thought it was wonderful that they were doing the hike at this stage of life. They would soon be furthering their education and getting on with life, but for now they were young and strong and on a big adventure.

I was not aware that they both were dealing with serious foot and leg problems that would eventually take them "off trail." Caribou first succumbed to recurring foot problems. I was surprised that Dovetail continued on alone since the two of them seemed inseparable. He did make new hiking companions and continued on, but he never seemed the same. Eventually he, too, had to forfeit the hike due to injuries and illness.

They are both in technical school now but do have plans to complete a thru-hike later in life. I know they have the character qualities that it takes to complete the trail. They survived the bitter cold of the Smokies, financial setbacks, unexpected medical bills, and severe pain with positive attitudes and contagious smiles. One day I believe they will complete the trail and earn the title thru-hiker.

If Caribou and Dovetail were the happiest hikers on the trail, then Rash was the friendliest and perhaps the most liked. Proverbs 18:24 states: "A man that has friends must show himself friendly" (AKJV). I don't know if Rash knew that verse, but he certainly lived it. Last time I looked, his trail journals had over 400,000 visits to them. Rash is a "good ole' country boy," but don't let that fool you. He is a very knowledgeable photographer, technology guru, and excellent writer, even if, as he says, "I need one heck of a spell checker."

Rash started his thru-hike in February. I first met him in Damascus, Virginia, nearly one-fourth of the way through the journey. I remember the encounter well because I instantly liked Rash. I think it is because he loves people and life. I had the privilege of hiking with Rash off and on through several states. At one point he got off trail for a week to visit his girlfriend and then returned to the trail. However, he was now out of his "bubble" of friends. Rash decided to abandon his thru-hike and yellow blaze (do the miles by car) ahead to rejoin them. He said that is when the real fun began. There was no pressure then, and he could relax and totally enjoy the journey. He and a couple of his friends also aqua blazed (kayaked) a portion of the trail. Several people criticized him on his journal for doing so, but Rash had been forthright that he was no longer pursuing a thru-hike. Rash's love for people and life meant more to him than one day having the coveted title of thru-hiker.

I kiddingly told Rash that everything he does ends with -in': huntin', fishin', hikin', and drinkin'. Due to his popularity, Rash had people waiting for him in trail towns wanting to buy him a drink and meet any of his needs. It was hard for him to get out of trail towns. Steve, a Trail Angel in Vermont, met Rash and me on the trail and served us grilled hamburgers, hot dogs, chips, cold beer, and Gatorade. Steve took me aside and told me he had been following Rash and me on our trail journals the entire journey. He said it was interesting to follow our journals and see our friendship develop. He shared that he would never have thought Rash and I would become hiking partners and friends because all I ever wrote about in my journal was God, and all Rash wrote about was beer!

Rash did summit Katahdin, not as a thru-hiker, but perhaps as the most popular and most liked hiker of 2013. He didn't quote or probably know the Bible verse on friendliness: he just lived it.

Nickelodian and Hoosier

Dovetail, Hoosier, Rash, Punkin Pie, Sparks, Mot, and Caribou (kneeling)

Shelter from the cold

Bail Bonds

There is a special bond with fellow thru-hikers. Tom, who has completed the AT and the PCT, mentioned that it is because we suffered the same things. That is so true. The hikers I am most connected to are those who started early and suffered through the brutal month of March in the Smokies. We froze but did so together. We also shared body heat in the shelters.

King David and Jonathan were very close. In his lament over Jonathan's death, David states that he loved Jonathan more than any woman. They were both warriors who had fought and suffered together, and that is the bond he is speaking of. Likewise, the Apostle Paul stated in Philippians 3:10 that he wanted to share in the sufferings of Christ. He knew that by doing so he would know, love, and appreciate Christ even more.

I remember a book about the Vietnam War titled *Friendships Forged In Battle*. It brought out the same truth: those who share in battle and its sufferings have a special bond. Although throughout my hike I looked forward to meeting and hiking with hikers I had not yet met on the trail, I doubted I would ever share the unique bond that developed on the trail with such hikers as Sparks, Joe the Hiker, Mot, Punkin Pie, GRRRR, Rash, Dovetail, Caribou, Nickelodian, Roadrunner, Z, Snowfrog, Bean, and Samson. We suffered together.

Joe the Hiker and Hoosier

Joe the Hiker

I first met Joe the Hiker in the early stages of the hike, when it was cold, really cold. Joe has a military background and is tough, but still, even he was suffering. We were in the same bubble and ended up at the same campsites at night. Soon Sparks, Joe the Hiker, and I began hiking together and sharing our life stories.

Joe had given himself the generic trail name Joe the Hiker because he wanted to be just a common, ordinary hiker on the AT. In his early fifties, Joe had recently completed a very successful corporate career. However, he had not been as successful in his family life. He was often away on business during major family events. A key reason for his taking the hike was to rethink life and his priorities. He shared that already he had decided things would be different when he returned home. His relationship with his family would now be a high priority.

Joe also opened up about his spiritual life. He said that he had been a committed "church man" most of his life and had participated in several mission trips but that his relationship with God needed to become a new priority as well. One of my highlights of the hike was sharing with Joe how he might have a close relationship with God through Jesus Christ. Joe committed himself to being a follower of Jesus Christ.

Not long after making that commitment, Joe announced that he was going home for a few days. His daughter had a recital where he wanted to make a surprise appearance. He also was going to treat his wife to a night at her favorite bed and breakfast. He did make the trip home and then returned to the trail and put in "big miles" in order to catch back up with me. Later in the Shenandoahs, Joe had several extended family members join him to hike short sections of the trail. Joe was accomplishing his new priorities even while on the trail. Joe was no longer hiking his own hike; this choice slowed his journey down to such an extent that he would not be able to complete the trail before needing to keep a prior commitment to help build a school in Belize with his home church for Habitat for Humanity. Joe would not return to the trail after the completion of the building project, which was a shock to anyone who knew him. However, a new Joe was emerging, one who valued close relationships and enjoyed the journey of life rather than one who was so goal driven. Joe did not accomplish a thru-hike on the AT, but he will on the trail of life.

Joe the Carpenter

One of my favorite hikers in the Bible is Joe the Carpenter, also known as the supposed father of Jesus, as the Bible states in Luke 3:23, but not much is written or known about him. We are told that he was a "just man" in Matthew 1:19. He was probably around twenty years old when he was chosen to be the father of Jesus; being chosen for such a task really changed his quiet life as a carpenter in the small, remote village of Nazareth. After the birth of Jesus, he had to flee, probably by foot, with his wife and baby eight hundred miles round trip to Egypt. He then settled in Nazareth.

As a carpenter he would be expected to teach carpentry to Jesus beginning at age twelve. The Gospel of Mark states that Jesus was also known as a carpenter. Interestingly, the original Greek word for carpenter, *tekton*, is a broad term meaning "a craftsman." It could be one who works with wood or stone. Many scholars believe that Joseph and Jesus were more likely stone masons since houses and most structures in the area were made of stone. Another reason is that at the time Joseph and Jesus lived in Nazareth, King Agrippa was rebuilding a beautiful Greco-Roman capital city named Sepphoris just three miles from Nazareth. Agrippa would have forcefully employed all quality *tektons* in the area to work on his Galilee capital city.

I have hiked from Nazareth to Sepphoris through fields, woods, and abandoned stone quarries where stones were quarried to rebuild the city. It is not easy terrain. It is very likely that Joseph hiked to Sepphoris and back six days a week to work. He would have been carrying his tools and food for the day in some sort of pack. I think Joseph would have related well to hikers. If he worked in Sepphoris, that means he hiked six miles a day, thirty-six miles a week, and 1,872 miles a year.

The last mention of Joseph in the Bible was when Jesus was twelve. Life was hard, and life expectancy was short. Life as a stone mason would have been especially hard. Joseph would have been very strong physically and a strong hiker. When we see depictions of Joseph, I think we should imagine him much like a thru-hiker, except with arms and shoulders unlike us scrawny-shouldered thru-hikers.

Maybe his trail name was Joe the Carpenter.

Carrying Burdens

I have referred to the benefits of slack packing and its spiritual application. In life we all need to carry our own load; we need to be responsible. However, we should also help others by helping them shoulder the load of life, especially when we see they are carrying a heavy burden. This is spoken about in

Galatians 6. I am certain there were times when Jesus helped someone carry his or her burden as He and His disciples walked the difficult and dusty paths of Israel. I am also certain there were people who asked Jesus if they could help carry His burden. Although not asked, Simon of Cyrene was told to do so by the Roman soldiers as Jesus carried the cross to Calvary. I bet it ended up being a highlight of his life (see Luke 22).

Samson

Samson, My Brother

Samson and I did well together. We both liked to get up around 5 A.M. and hike until around 5 P.M. We liked to swim in rivers and lakes, take breaks often, and stealth camp near streams. Instead of pushing for big miles, we just hiked until late afternoon and began looking for a stream where we could stealth camp. The stream provided a bath, a water source, and thankfully, a cover for Samson's snoring. (Twice people thought a bear was in the camp, but it was Samson snoring.)

After the hike I had a speaking engagement about the hike at a retreat center in the Black Hills. Samson flew in from Mississippi and spoke along with me. After the retreat, he and I spent almost a week hiking the Black Hills of South Dakota. The park was abandoned—we had it to ourselves. One of the highlights of the trip was "cowboy camping" under the stars on a moonlit, crystal-clear night in the desolate beauty of the Badlands. It was awesome, especially experiencing it with a good friend. Someone has said that "a shared joy is a double joy, and a shared sorrow is half a sorrow." On this hike the joy was double, and there was no sorrow.

It wasn't always that way for Samson and me. We shared many difficult days on the trail. However, walking through them together is what fostered such a close relationship. We have what I call a David and Jonathan relationship. David and Jonathan were both committed to the God of Israel. They were also soldiers who fought a common enemy for the survival of the nation of Israel and the glory of their God.

Samson and I are both followers of Jesus striving to glorify Him with our lives as we serve as soldiers of the Cross. Samson is truly my brother—I think we would both say that we are a gift from God to each other and that we are friends for life.

God's Hand

Each morning of my hike, I read the Psalm that corresponded to the number of days since I started the hike. In Psalm 139:5, the writer states that God hemmed him in, behind, and before and that God's hand was upon him. I experienced that protection on the trail in a unique, memorable way only a few days after reading it.

When coming down an extremely steep section of Mount Moosilauke in the White Mountains of New Hampshire, Samson was following just a few steps behind me. Now Samson is big: around 6'3", and even as a scrawny thru-hiker, he weighed around 185. Suddenly Samson lost his footing and fell forward, landing on me. My feet flew out from underneath me, and I slid several feet down the mountain on my pack. I had stopped Samson's fall; however, I distinctly remember a hand grabbing my pack so that I did not fall face-first to disaster. After getting back up, I thanked Samson for grabbing me. He said that he was totally out of control and did not grab me. We both concluded that a guardian angel or God Himself had done so.

I know Psalm 139:5 is true by experience. I also know I don't want Samson or anyone else hiking that close behind me in the future.

Earning the View

Two friends Brian and Rick joined me to hike forty miles of The White Mountains in New Hampshire, and it was fun watching

Rick, Hoosier, and Brian

them enjoy the hike. It far exceeded their expectations in both difficulty and enjoyment. The views were difficult to attain but well worth the climb. They both commented that life is like that as well: we seem to appreciate most what we have to work for. If we could have taken a helicopter to the top of the mountains, the views would not have been nearly as rewarding. It seems God has designed life so that we truly appreciate only what we have worked hard to achieve.

TRAVELING RIGHT: FOLLOWING THE WHITE BLAZES

80,000 Signs

The Appalachian Trail is actually very easy to follow. There are approximately eighty thousand white blazes on trees, logs, fence posts, or rocks along the trail. Also, the trail itself is generally pretty evident. However, there are side trails that are called blue blaze trails, which lead to other destinations along the way. AT "purists" will not blue blaze; they stay only on the Appalachian Trail.

In 2007 in the White Mountains, I blue blazed around Mount Madison due to a storm, only to get lost. I fell down a cliff during a storm and got laid up in Gorham, New Hampshire, for a couple days. I found out later that I was on one of the most dangerous trails in the White Mountains during a storm. To make the matter worse, I was alone with no one to help me.

Jesus had a chance to blue blaze when He was in the Garden of Gethsemane. He said in Matthew 26:39, "My Father, if it be possible, let this cup pass from me; nevertheless, not as I will, but as you will." Jesus chose to stay true to the will of God rather than take any other trail to accomplish the course set out for Him. The Apostle Paul states in II Timothy 4:7: "... I have fought THE good fight, I have finished THE course, I have kept THE faith" [emphasis added] (ASV). He is very specific that he was true to the course laid out by God. They were spiritual purists.

Star Blazing

The Christmas story states that the Magi followed a particular star on their journey of perhaps eight hundred miles to Bethlehem. Many scholars believe they were astrologers from Persia who were familiar with an ancient prophesy about a unique star rising over Israel, indicating that a child had been born who would become a glorious king. The Magi believed that the child had already been born, that God had announced it in the heavens, and that they had come to worship Him. After arriving at Jerusalem where they assumed the new king would be, they found that another prophecy said the king would be born in Bethlehem, the hometown of David. They left Jerusalem for the six-mile journey to Bethlehem, and "the star that they had seen when it rose went before them until it came to rest over the place where the child was. When they saw the star, they rejoiced exceedingly with great joy" (Matthew 2:9-10).

Many generations before Jesus, David, the ancient shepherd/king of Israel, followed the white blazes of God's word to give him direction for life. In Psalm 119:105 he writes, "Show me your ways, Lord, teach me your paths. Guide me in your truth and teach me" (25:4-5a NIV). "Your word is a lamp for my feet, a light on my path" (119:105 NIV).

I, too, have found the "blazes" giving direction for life found in the Bible are much like the blazes on the AT. Following them proves to be the right path and will lead to a wonderful destination.

Spring Goeth Before My Fall

Hiking over Dragon's Tooth Mountain proved very difficult and demanded extreme care. I did not fall going over it because I "walked circumspectly." Later, however, I was not being careful since the trail was smooth and easy to hike. Suddenly, I tripped over a small root and had a really hard fall.

I reflected upon this and realized that spiritually we usually fall when we are overly confident and not being careful. We need to be walking through life carefully, wisely, or circumspectly, with our eyes wide open, as the King James Version says in Ephesians 5:15.

Lack of Direction

Upon leaving Harpers Ferry, West Virginia, the trail follows alongside the Potomac River on a tow path for several miles. The hiking is easy, but the trail is very poorly marked. White blazes are rare. After not seeing a white blaze for over a half mile, I backtracked to see if I had somehow gotten off the trail. That amounted to over a mile of wasted walking. Later the same thing happened again. It was very frustrating. When I finally saw a white blaze, I lifted my hiking poles high into the air praising God that I was on the right path.

It is also very frustrating in life not to have direction. In Psalm 119 the psalmist repeatedly praises God for His word, which gives direction for life. It is the longest of the 150 Psalms. I can almost see the writer lifting his shepherd's staff into the air and praising God for direction.

Feline Conversation Matters

An interesting conversation takes place between Alice and the Cat in *Alice in Wonderland*. "Alice, upon coming to a fork in the road, asks the Cat, 'Would you tell me, please, which way I ought to go from here?'

'That depends a good deal on where you want to get to,' the Cat says.

'I don't much care where—' replies Alice.

'Then it doesn't matter which way you go,' says the Cat."[2]

AT thru-hikers come to forks on the trail. Since they are committed to reaching Katahdin, it matters greatly to them which way they go. Life itself is a pilgrimage for all of us. If we desire to travel well and arrive at our desired destination, then it is of great importance which way we go. I have found following Jesus and His teachings to be the best road to travel and recommend it to all fellow pilgrims. It matters!

Stop and Reflect

"Stand at the crossroads and look; ask for the ancient paths, ask where the good way is, and walk in it, and you will find rest for your souls" (NIV). These words from Jeremiah 6:16 are worthy of serious reflection. To stand is a summons to a traveler to stop and think about his or her journey. We as travelers of life often come to a crossroads.

At such times, it is important to stop, stand, and ask ourselves some serious questions, such as how is the journey going? Where is this path taking me? Is this the path I want to remain on? We should also ask those who are traveling well where the ancient (eternal) paths are. Walking those ancient paths will, with time, prove to be the good paths that bring rest to weary souls. AT hikers know how important it is to stay on the path marked out by white blazes. Followers of Jesus have found that the ancient paths blazed in the Bible are the paths that prove to be "the good way," so we should commit to traveling those paths.

TRAIL BLIGHT: CHALLENGES ALONG THE WAY

The Month I Was Cold

I describe March as "the month I was cold." Long before arriving in the Smokies, we heard frightful stories of temperatures in the single digits, fifty mile-per-hour winds, thunderstorms, sleet, snow, three-to-four-foot drifts, and miles of trail that had turned into a river of ice. It all proved to be true—there was no exaggeration. Peaks in the Smoky Mountains are often over five and even six thousand feet above sea level, and three-and-a-half degrees are lost per thousand feet elevation gain. We were typically in our sleeping bags huddled up against each other like sardines in a can for warmth from dusk until dawn. Our water bottles were frozen in the morning. We had to beat our frozen boots against the shelter wall in order to get our feet in them. Often we could not tie our boots since the boot strings were frozen solid as well. It wasn't worth freezing to prepare breakfast, so we generally just started hiking and eating power bars as we walked. All energy was used to try to stay warm. I came out of the Smokies having lost at least twenty pounds, but I was not alone in the misery. Hundreds of miles later there was a special bond when meeting someone I "survived the Smokies" with. We were later told that 2013 would go down in history as the coldest March in the Smokies in over forty years. It was amazing to think that we got to be a part of such a historic event.

We have all heard the expression "misery loves company." That may be true, but I would add, "You love the company you go through misery with." So although the month of March was miserable in many ways and I would not want to repeat it, it was a bonding experience with other hikers that I would not trade for a sunny and pleasant March.

Fear Is a Four-Letter Word

Before entering the six-thousand-foot Smokies, it was interesting listening to others talk about them. The best word to describe the mountains is fear, not because of the terrain but the weather conditions, which can change in a minute. However, there is an expression on the trail that "if you don't walk in the rain, you'll never make it to Maine."

The seventy-two-mile stretch known as the Smokies *are* to be feared. A storm hit while we were going over Thunderhead Mountain: winds were probably forty to fifty miles per hour, and it was raining. We arrived at our shelter before the full force of the storm hit and found four students from Tufts University inside. When Roadrunner from Germany showed up, it was hailing and raining fiercely. Then GRRRR showed up cold, wet, and in the early stages of hypothermia. The Smokies were showing their stuff, but we found a shelter from the storm.

While hiking through the Smokies, I kept thinking of all the Bible passages that speak of God being our shelter in the storms of life. One of my favorite passages regarding this is found in Isaiah 32, which foretells the time when the King (Jesus) reigns in righteousness, and justice will be like a shelter from the wind and a refuge from the storm. A great lesson thus far is that Jesus is our safety and our protection and should be the place of shelter we pursue each day. Likewise, in Psalm 27:5a David states, "God will hide me in his shelter in the day of trouble."

It is interesting that the most-repeated command in the scriptures is "Do not fear." That must be because God knows we are so prone to being afraid. Later in the same Psalm David says, "be strong, and let your heart take courage." I prefer that over fear.

Groan Mountain

Ephesians 5:15 states that we ought to "look carefully then how [we] walk, not as unwise but as wise . . . because the days are evil." One day in Tennessee, we were making great time over Roan Mountain, which hikers call "Groan Mountain," when suddenly we realized it was going to take more time than expected. The snow had melted and turned into a frozen river of ice. Around three miles of the trail over the mountain was "evil"! Every step had to be planned and taken carefully. Joe the Hiker, Sparks, and I fell several times. Thankfully, although beaten up, we were not injured.

That day reminded me of the passage in Ephesians because of how slippery life can be at times. We need to be very careful how we walk . . . that is, how we live our lives. The book of Ephesians further says we ought to walk in love (5:2) as children of the light (5:8) and worthy of our calling as Christians (4:1). Walking over Roan Mountain demanded very careful attention, and so does life.

Still, even while walking carefully, we all fall. We see throughout Scripture that many of the great characters who loved God fell at times in their spiritual lives, too. Yet, as it states in Proverbs 24:16: " . . . for though the righteous fall seven times, they rise again" (NIV). We kept getting back up and made it to over "Groan Mountain" beaten up but unbroken.

Faith in the Fog

There were times on the Trail when I could not see fifty feet due to heavy fog. It made it very difficult to see the white blazes showing where the trail was. Philip Yancey writes about a man who swam out into a lake one evening, when suddenly fog rolled in, and he became totally disoriented. He was petrified until he heard a familiar voice. He swam toward the familiar voice, which led him to shore.[3]

II Corinthians 5:7 states "we walk by faith, not by sight." That was literally true hiking through the dense fog, but it is also true in our spiritual lives.

Thomas said in John 20:25, "Unless I see the nail marks in his hands and put my finger where the nails were, and put my hand into his side, I will not believe" (NIV).

"Jesus said to him, 'Put your finger here; see my hands. Reach out your hand and put it into my side. Stop doubting and believe.'

Thomas said to him, 'My Lord and my God!'

Then Jesus told him, 'Because you have seen me, you have believed; blessed are those who have not seen and yet have believed' " (John 20:27-29 NIV).

Trail Blight: Challenges Along the Way

Out here I have thought about the fact that I want to live by faith and not by sight. I want to experience Him as my Lord and God by faith.

Rocksylvania

Every thru-hiker was saying the same thing: "I can't wait to get out of Pennsylvania." It's the rocks. My new boots lasted three days, just sixty miles before the rocks cut the rubber toe up. No wonder Pennsylvania is called "the state where boots go to die."

While I was stepping through Pennsylvania on day ninety-four, I was reading Psalm 94 verse 18, which states, "When I said my foot is slipping, your unfailing love, Lord, supported me" (NIV). On the eighteenth day, Psalm 18 addressed this same theme: verse 33 states, "He made my feet like the feet of a deer and set me secure on the heights," and verse 36 reads, "You gave a wide place for my steps under me, and my feet did not slip."

It takes only one misstep out of over five million to join the ranks of the injured who were off the trail due to leg, ankle, and foot problems from the Pennsylvania rocks taking their toll. All these hikers made it through the brutal winter in the Smokies; they are tough hikers. It was only by the grace of God that I remained on the trail. I asked God to enlarge my path, help me not to slip, get me up the high places, and give me the feet of a deer. I hiked most of Pennsylvania alone, and my feet got pretty bruised along the way.

Pennsylvania is a part of everyone's life journey. We all face lonely, difficult, and painful times. However, there is no way to reach our goal, our spiritual Mount Katahdin, without going through challenging times. In Acts 14, Paul encourages the believers in Antioch, Iconium, and Lystra to continue in the faith and reminds them that only through many hardships shall we enter the kingdom of God.

I have had the privilege of hiking the seventeen miles from Iconium to Lystra in modern-day Turkey. It is not easy terrain and even today is a dangerous place due to wolves. John Mark turned back from going there. Paul did not turn back and was stoned in Lystra and left for dead. However, it is also where he met Timothy, his son in the faith. Good came out of extreme difficulty.

I believe that was the take-away for me from Pennsylvania. Only by going through the hardships of Pennsylvania could I have reached Mount Katahdin and accomplished the goal of becoming a thru-hiker.

There is no avoiding Pennsylvania—it is a part of the designated trail. There is no avoiding the difficulties of life, either. It is part of our journey, and only by going through them will we reach the goal of being a faithful follower of Jesus Christ.

Mahoosuc Notch and Arm

I made it through the notorious Mahoosuc Notch and Arm in western Maine. The Notch is known as the most difficult mile of the trail: it is a jumbled mess of rocks and boulders in a notch between two mountains and takes a couple hours to make it through. That stretch is difficult enough, but it was raining and cold the morning I worked my way through it. There were still ice and snow in the notch, so I took a beating and came out cold and soaked at 11 A.M. I made it through—and I was through. I set up my tent, crawled into my damp sleeping bag, and didn't wake up until the next morning only to find it was cold and rainy again.

Trail Blight: Challenges Along the Way

After the Notch came the Arm, a one-mile steep granite slab that is particularly dangerous when wet. I made it up the Arm and hiked another mile and a half to Speck Pond and Shelter; Speck Pond is the highest body of water in Maine. A caretaker at the shelter greeted me and saw my condition. He told me to set up my tent and get in my sleeping bag, and he would bring me coffee and something hot to eat. Later he told me I appeared to be on the edge of hypothermia. I spent the day and night in my tent. Although it was mid-summer, it was only in the high thirties at night.

I hiked only five miles in two days. I had not planned on it taking so long to get to the next town for supplies, so besides being fatigued, I was also out of food and fuel. I resorted to begging for necessities. I asked for food from two Franciscan priests who were out for a few days and for fuel from a Boy Scout troop who was out for a few days. They were all accommodating, which was kind. It was a humbling experience—I was supposed to know what I was doing after hiking over 1,900 miles.

In the past, I could never figure out how someone could come this far on the trail and then quit. Now I understand. New Hampshire and Maine are tough. Tired thru-hikers often say they are ready to "finish this thang!" I had never thought of quitting, but I must admit I was tired. I decided to take the next day off since I needed a break from the trail. Even Jesus told His disciples to cross over the Sea of Galilee to get away from the crowds and to get some needed rest. I wonder if they had food . . . no problem with Jesus around, though; He multiplied fish and bread and turned water to wine. I instead hit up priests and Boy Scouts!

Rat Good Train

I heard the story of a southern girl thru-hiker who kept talking about "rat good train." A couple other hikers were confused until they realized she was saying "right-good terrain." Even that is a bit confusing because the AT offers very little right-good terrain. From Georgia to Maine, it seems hikers are always dealing with difficult terrain. Roan Mountain was a frozen river of ice, the Smokies had snow drifts three feet deep, Virginia had the green tunnel, Pennsylvania the cutting rocks, Vermont the muck, New Hampshire the boulders, and Maine the roots. It was seldom "rat-good train."

It seems life is much like that as well, with little right-good terrain. Seldom is life like a walk in the park. Who ever said it would or should be? In Acts 14:22 the Apostle Paul, after being stoned and left for dead, returned to the same city he was stoned in. He encouraged the believers there to keep on believing and not to be discouraged because it is "through many tribulations must we enter into the kingdom of God." The Greek word translated *tribulation* was used in that day for the crushing of grapes to make wine. The only way we get to Katahdin or the kingdom is though "rat-**tough** train," but then we have the joy of reaching Katahdin and the kingdom and becoming fine wine rather than dried-up raisins.

Hikers' Hobble

I recently saw a billboard for an urgent care center. In bold letters it said, "Walk-ins and Limp-ins Welcome." I don't know that it would have caught my attention like it did if I had not just completed a very long walk (and if I weren't still limping from it). Several thru-hikers I know also experienced "hikers' hobble" since accomplishing the thru-hike. It seems the hike took a toll on all of our joints.

Jacob limped. He was named Jacob, which means "to grasp" since at birth he was grasping at his twin brother's heel, trying to pull himself ahead. In the book of Genesis, it is recorded that he lived up to his name, always doing anything necessary to get ahead. However, one night he had a wrestling match with God, and they both won. Jacob walked away a winner, blessed by God, and given a new name. But, he was limping; God had also won. God had won over the heart of Jacob to such a degree that he was a new man and deserved a new name. His new "trail name" *Israel* roughly translates to "One who struggles with God, prevails, and becomes a Prince of God."

I would like to think that to have the hikers' hobble is an honor. Thru-hikers have earned the stiff, sore joints because they have gone through a great struggle and have prevailed. I am grateful that God, like the urgent care center, welcomes those who limp along through life, struggling with and seeking to become a Prince of God.

SPIRITUAL MIGHT: LONGING FOR THE SPIRITUAL CONNECTIONS

Modern-Day Pilgrims

People hike the AT for various reasons. An official and popular statement is that the AT is "a footpath for those seeking fellowship with the wilderness." That was certainly true for the hikers I met and for me, but for many of us, there was more that drew us to the trail.

For many, the hike was a spiritual pilgrimage. We were seeking a closer relationship with God, the Creator of the wilderness. One of my favorite Psalms is Psalm 84, which speaks of the pilgrims of Israel who hiked to Jerusalem in order to worship at the Temple three times a year. For Jesus and His parents, it was a three- or four-day, seventy-mile journey from Nazareth to Jerusalem (see Luke 2:41-52). Verse 5 of the Psalm reads, "Blessed are those whose strength is in you, whose hearts are set on pilgrimage" (NIV).

A pilgrimage is more than a journey: although it has a beginning and destination, the purpose of the journey has a spiritual goal in mind. The travelers on their way to Jerusalem were seeking God. There are people who see themselves as tourists, here primarily to enjoy life. Some see life as a struggle to endure and overcome. Others see it as a competition, striving to reach a goal ahead of others and be the "winners." Pilgrims see themselves as people on a journey, headed toward a destination, with a compelling desire to develop a growing relationship with God and other pilgrims.

The Condition of Your Sole

Hikers are obsessed with the condition of their feet. Many of us suffered from bad blisters and bruising on the bottoms of our feet. I understand now how beating the bottom of a person's feet is a form of punishment in some countries. It is painful. I have seen hikers completely duct tape their feet in order to continue their hike.

The New Testament records over thirteen thousand miles of the Apostle Paul's journeys, which were mostly on foot. He did so in order to spread the message of Jesus throughout the Roman world. He didn't have Merino wool socks, Gore-Tex boots with Vibram soles, or duct tape. I assume he wore the best shoes or sandals available at the time. Still, I'm sure he often suffered from foot problems. He never mentions the condition of his feet but rather his purpose in walking. He writes in Ephesians 6 that followers of Jesus should have their feet shod with readiness to share the good news of peace with God through Jesus Christ. As Paul traveled and preached, he also strove to live a life that would draw people to his message. Many years later Saint Francis of Assisi spoke of the importance of a winsome life as well when he stated that "walking to preach is useless unless our walking is preaching."

Legging It

I was hustling through the ancient streets of Jerusalem trying to find the bus station in order to catch a bus to Nazareth, the boyhood home of Jesus. I was in Israel to hike The Jesus Trail, a historic hiking trail meandering through ancient Galilee where Jesus lived and walked two thousand years ago. I asked a young man in a military uniform if he spoke English. He shook his head. From behind me, I heard a female voice with a British accent say, "I speak English; can I help you?"

I turned and saw an attractive red-haired young woman in her mid-twenties. I explained to her my need to find the bus station.

"Are you legging it?" she asked.

Confused, I asked, "What?"

She repeated herself, "Are you legging it?" and tapped her leg.

"Oh, yes," I said, "I am legging it."

"Then follow me. I'm legging it there," she said.

I hadn't heard the expression "legging it" before but have since been told it is a common expression in England for walking briskly.

We are all legging it somewhere and following someone. It is crucial that we are on the right path and following the right person so that we arrive at the right destination. What benefits us is taking time out to consider whether we are walking the right path, following the right person, and arriving at the right destination in our journey of life.

One Anothers

I was laid up for forty-eight hours giving my leg a rest in a trail-town motel. However, I was not alone. There were probably twenty hikers, many injured, in the motel I was staying in. Although we were not on the trail, there was a special bond between us: we were all a part of the trail community.

It reminds me of the community of faith. In the community of faith, we should be seeing the "one anothers" as they are called of scripture. Here are just a few: to love, honor, encourage, respect, and accept one another. These are a given in the hiking community. May we see them as dominant features of the faith community, too.

Moxie Mary

I read that approximately twenty percent of thru-hikers are female. I had the privilege of meeting and hiking with a few of them and found them to be tough, tenacious hikers. I met female hikers with the trail names of Gummy Bear, Camaro, Coffee Pot, Foxy, Wild Rain, Breitside, Hobbit, Lady Gray, Lil' Sas, and Moxie. I know other male hikers would agree that they *all* had moxie, defined as the ability to face difficulty with courage, spirit, and skill.

Mary, the mother of Jesus, had moxie. She was probably around fifteen years old when she went to see her aunt Elizabeth. Luke writes, "Mary arose and went with haste into the hill country, to a town in Judah" (Luke 1:39). We are not told how she traveled or what town she went to, but most scholars would agree that she probably went by foot and that the trip was around one hundred miles. Luke later writes in Luke 1:56, "Mary remained with [Elizabeth] about three months and returned to her home," another one hundred miles.

Then we have the familiar Christmas story in which she travels over one hundred miles from Nazareth to Bethlehem, probably by donkey due to her pregnancy. After the birth of Jesus, she and Joseph settled in Bethlehem. However, within two years they had to flee at night, probably by foot, four hundred miles to Egypt. Sometime later they returned to Nazareth, again probably by foot, another four hundred miles. When Jesus was twelve years old, Mary made a two-hundred-mile round-trip journey to Jerusalem for the feast of Passover. Luke 2:41 says she "went to Jerusalem every year at the Feast of the Passover."

During Jesus' ministry we find her walking with Jesus all over the rough and rocky hills of Israel. Mary was one tough, tenacious female hiker with moxie. I think her trail name is given in the Bible as well. In the *Magnificat*, found in Luke 1:48, she says, "from now on all generations will call me blessed."

Discipleship Defined

Three section-hikers joined me for a week of hiking in Virginia. One is a longtime friend of mine, and the other two are her friends and now my new friends. I was so proud of them: they joined me at a difficult section and hiked two four-thousand-foot steep mountains on their first day. Even the thru-hikers were sharing with them what a hard section they had their first day. They slept in tents through cold rainy nights, hiked through thick fog and rain, and even hitched into a trail town. They were having a blast and so was I as I watched them learning about and living out trail life. They spent an evening sitting around a campfire talking to thru-hikers and catching "hiker fever."

It reminds me of what the Bible calls discipleship. I believe we are meant to find the same joy in introducing others to the path of following Jesus and seeing them follow Him. The best definition of discipleship I have heard is listening, learning, and then living as a follower of Jesus. Two of these hikers only months later joined in hiking the Jesus Trail in Israel.

Thru-Hiking, Shepherd Style

I was once asked what biblical character I most related to in the Christmas story. I immediately responded that it was the shepherds, which I assume would be the response of most thru-hikers. The gospel of Luke says that shepherds were "out in the fields." They lived under the sun, moon, and stars as they cared for their sheep. Luke goes on to say that that they were "keeping watch over their flocks by night." It was a dangerous and lonely job being a shepherd. Some shepherds lost their lives fighting off predators, and thieves were always lurking in the shadows hoping to steal from the flock.

The well-known shepherd David stated that he had killed a lion and a bear while protecting his flock. Shepherds, like thru-hikers, spent months at a time living outside, so they were usually dirty and smelled like sheep. They were even considered "unclean" spiritually since their jobs kept them from attending synagogue services. Shepherds were constantly on the move as they led their sheep to new pastures. Perhaps others even labeled them "shepherd trash." They did, like thru-hikers, enjoy living in community with other shepherds outside in God's creation and seemed to be special to God. After all, it was shepherds alone who received the special visitation by angels and the invitation to go to Bethlehem to see the baby Jesus who was born to "shepherd His people." Priests and kings were not invited, just a few stinky shepherds. They didn't seem to be surprised that the baby was born in a barn and lying in an animal feeding trough. Their own children's births would have been similar.

Luke states that the shepherds told everyone what they had heard and seen that night and that everyone "wondered at what the shepherds told them" (Luke 2:18). I wonder if the shepherds had any idea that the baby would grow up and be known as the Good Shepherd who would lay down His life for His sheep.

Getting My Note Right

I especially like Psalm 148. In it the Psalmist calls all creation to praise God. I have thought about God and His creation quite a bit out here. Like an artist's art, God's creation says much about Him. He is the creator, He is powerful, and He loves variety and beauty.

In Psalm 150 a call is made for all creation and various instruments to praise Him. He wants all creation, all that has life and breath, to give Him praise. Why, is He needy or insecure? No, He deserves it. At the end of the Psalm, there is a command that we humans should praise Him as well. It seems only we humans have a choice in the matter. When we catch a glimpse of who He is, praise will come naturally. It is more than words of praise, though—it is to be the complete expression of our lives. I know most of the time I am like an off-key instrument, making an irritable sound, but every once in a while I get a note right as His instrument. It is then I sense most His pleasure and fulfillment in being what I was meant to be. It is time to get back on the trail, see His creation, and try to get my note right in His orchestra.

Cubicle Hikers

In August, I took time off from my thru-hike so that I could speak at a conference. Afterward, I was anxious to get back on the AT. Speaking at a conference about the trail is not the same as hiking it. It is easy to read, study, speak, and write about a subject and somehow get the false impression that I experienced it. I have heard from other hikers that they have been harassed on their trail journal by what they call "cubicle hikers" who negatively critique their hike. Thankfully, I have received very little of that. I think those who have the right to critique are those who are out there on the trail facing the same challenges.

The same holds true for our walk with God. It is so easy to study, develop, and defend our particular theology, read various authors, go to church and Bible studies, and somehow think that is the essence of living the Christian life. All these activities are good but are not in themselves a walk, which is what the Christian life is described as.

Spiritually we also need to crawl out of our cubicles and get into the dirt and mud of life.

The Journey of a Lifetime

Walking the Appalachian Trail made me wonder how far Jesus walked during His time on Earth. Thankfully, a man named Arthur Blessitt has already done the research. Blessitt is quite a walker himself. He holds the Guinness Record for the world's longest walk: he has walked over forty thousand miles carrying a twelve-foot cross. He claims from his studies of the Gospels that Jesus walked more than 21,000 miles. Jesus' earliest long walk is believed to be the four-hundred-mile trip back to Nazareth from Egypt when He was perhaps five or six years old.

Whatever the cumulative distance, we do know that He is constantly seen walking many miles over difficult terrain throughout the Gospels.

Christians celebrate the Son of God leaving Heaven, coming to Earth, and becoming flesh. How far was that journey? His hardest walk was less than a mile from Pilate's headquarters in Jerusalem to Calvary outside the city gates. He was able to slack pack as Simon of Cyrene was forced to carry His cross. Followers of Jesus believe that He rose from the dead, walked the earth for forty days, ascended into Heaven, and will one day return to once again walk upon the earth as King.

Now that's a thru-hike.

w

The *Appalachian Trail Thru-Hikers' Companion* uses a lower-case w as the symbol for water. A capital *W* is the symbol for the direction west.[4] Although it was very important to have my directions correct on the trail, having water was crucial. My daily hiking plan was heavily influenced by where water would be available, perhaps from a spring, stream, pond, or lake. Springs and streams were preferable; water from ponds and lakes was suspect and should be filtered, treated, or boiled. I usually hydrated at the source, which means I drank as much as I could at the stream or spring, and carried as little water as possible due to weight: water weighs eight pounds a gallon. However, water was so vital that at times I carried a gallon and filtered water from mud puddles when the situation demanded it.

Thinking about water caused me to reflect upon an event in Jesus' life from a thru-hiker's perspective. In John 4 (according to Hoosier), Jesus and His disciples were hiking back home in Galilee from Jerusalem in Judea, a hike of around sixty miles over rough terrain. It was very hot, around noon, and they were out of food and water. They were hiking through Samaria and were less than a mile from a town named Sychar. Samaria was not hiker friendly, and Sychar was no trail town. Still, Jesus was hot, tired, thirsty, and without food. He told His disciples to go into town to buy food while He rested by a well. He was really thirsty but had no way of getting water out of the deep well. A woman came to draw water, but she was a Samaritan woman and He a male Jew. She certainly was not a likely Trail Angel. However, He asked her to draw Him some water from the well, but instead she wanted to talk about their religious differences. Jesus told her that if she knew whom she was talking to, she would ask Him for the water He had to offer, living (flowing, pure) water. She finally recognized Him as a prophet and ran to town just as the disciples arrived with food. She returned with a crowd from Sychar, Jesus and His disciples were offered trail magic from the whole town, and they ended up taking two zeroes there. While there, He continued talking about living water until they finally realized He was speaking about spiritual thirst and was offering a drink from the "well of salvation that never will run dry" and will satisfy the thirst of their souls. She had been trying to quench the thirst of her soul through men—she had been through five marriages and was currently living with a guy. They had a wonderful time in Sychar before Jesus and His disciples continued on their journey. They arrived home in Galilee with fond memories of their time in Sychar, which was now full of Trail Angels.

The Sentry

The story goes that a first-century rabbi was walking after dark and being deep in thought, took a wrong turn. Without realizing it, he came upon a sentry guarding a Roman military outpost. Hearing footsteps, the sentry yelled, "Who goes there, and where are you going?" The rabbi did not reply. Again, the sentry yelled out even louder, "Who goes there, and where are you going?"

This time the rabbi called back, "I am a rabbi who took a wrong turn, but how much do you get paid for asking those questions?"

"Ten denarii a day," the sentry gruffly replied. "Why?"

The Rabbi responded, "Because I will pay you double your salary if you stand outside my door and ask me those same questions each morning."

The wise rabbi realized how important it is to know who we are and where we are going in life. It is also very important on the AT to remember that we are thru-hikers and headed to Katahdin. Trail names are helpful as they are constant reminders of who we are and define our new identity on the trail. It is also crucial that each morning as thru-hikers break camp and hit the trail that we get back on the right path, go in the right direction, and remember our destination. Off trail the same holds true. We must remember who we are, stay on the right path, and keep focused on our ultimate destination.

Crutch

Most thru-hikers I met along the trail used hiking sticks or poles. Some started out without them but later began using at least one hiking stick. I do know some hikers who did not use poles or sticks, and I admire their sure-footedness. However, most hikers would agree that using at least one hiking stick gave them assurance, took considerable stress off their knees, and saved them from many falls.

I believe this principle has a spiritual parallel. Some call religion a "crutch." I accept that. For a person walking through the rough terrain of life, it seems wise to have someone to lean upon for strength, stability, and support. Perhaps worse than needing a crutch would be needing one but not having one. Solomon, the ancient wise king of Israel, wrote in Proverbs 3:5-6, "Trust [put your weight upon] in the LORD with all your heart and lean not on [don't put your weight upon] your own understanding; in all your ways submit to him [seek His strength, stability, and counsel], and he will make your paths straight" (NIV).

So on the trail, I use hiking poles. And on the trail of life, I use and recommend the "crutch" of a relationship with God. He has given me assurance, removed stress, and saved me from many falls.

It Is Finished

On Good Friday from noon until 3:00, Sparks and I were going up a very difficult bald called Big Bald. During the tedious three hours, Sparks and I went over and discussed the words of Jesus from the cross. Just as we accomplished the climb, I looked at my watch, which read 3 P.M. I looked at Sparks and said, "It is finished!"

We accomplished our climb.

His climb up Golgotha accomplished our salvation.

Hiker Trash

I stopped into a hamburger joint the other day and saw a homeless guy sitting in a corner. I felt strangely drawn to him, almost like I'd seen a friend. He looked like "hiker trash."

Thru-hikers are actually quite fond of the moniker "hiker trash" and often refer to ourselves as such. Although we've known trail towns and Trail Angels who have treated us like celebrities and seemed not to notice our filth and stench, we have felt like trash when attempting to hitch a ride along trash-strewn ditches to unfriendly towns and have seen eyes that stare straight through us sitting at lonely seats in the back corners of restaurants. The homeless guy had food and a cup of coffee, so I didn't buy him anything. I did, however, catch his eye and acknowledge him. He stared back and smiled slightly. Nothing was said verbally, yet much was communicated. Somehow, I think he knew that I knew and understood.

Looking at the birth of Jesus, now there is a hiker trash story. There was no room in the inn, so He was born in a barn. I have been in those "barns" in Bethlehem. They are actually animal stalls in a rock cave-like structure. The stench is awful, and it is filthy. Just think, the first family of Christmas was a hiker trash family. Joseph had just hiked over one hundred miles. Mary most probably had ridden a donkey for the last three to four days—while very pregnant. As heavenly angels sang, stinky shepherds wiped the manure off their sandals and stuck their heads into the cave to stare in stark wonder. The religious leaders stayed in the temple going through their rituals and missed the whole thing. Paranoid King Herod partied with political leaders in his luxurious palace while sending soldiers five miles to the small village of Bethlehem to kill the baby Jesus.

Today many still consider Jesus hiker trash, but I feel strangely drawn to Him, almost like I've seen a friend.

(Paraphrasing Parenthetically)

I love how Hebrews 12:1-2 in *The Message* reads and how it relates to being a spiritual and physical thru-hiker. I quoted it here with a few of "Hoosier's Reflections" in parentheses.

Chapter 11 is a list of spiritual thru-hikers of the faith who successfully completed their journey. Chapter 12 then states, "Do you see what this means—all these pioneers who blazed the way" (people can be white blazes along life's trail, showing us the way. For example, Roadrunner broke trail through the snowdrifts of the Smokies in bitterly cold and snowy conditions), "all these veterans cheering us on?" (One asset to the AT is that there is no competition: everyone is pulling for the other to make it to Katahdin.) "It means we'd better get on with it." (If they could do it, so can we!) "Strip down" (lose weight—both physically and pack-wise, get rid of the extras, non-essentials), "start running—" (walking, for us—get moving, take that first step), "and never quit" (not even on a sunny day). "No extra spiritual fat, no parasitic sins" (surrender to a spiritual shakedown).

"Keep your eyes on Jesus, who both began and finished this race" (hike) "we're in." (Jesus is our ultimate example of how to hike through life.) "Study how he did it. Because he never lost sight of where he was headed—that exhilarating finish in and with God—" (although we walk through life one step at a time, we need to keep the end in mind. Don't hang out too long in trail towns, get back on trail, stay focused, and remember, you are a thru-hiker) "he could put up with anything along the way: Cross, shame, whatever" (sleet, snow, rain, roots, cold, heat, bugs, bogs, boulders, blisters, snakes, stench, snoring, whatever). "And now he's there, in the place of honor, right alongside God." (He is THE GOD-MAN THRU-HIKER.)

"When you find yourselves flagging in your faith" (feeling you cannot complete the journey), "go over that story again, item by item, that long litany of hostility he plowed through" (obscene gestures from people in cars when hitch-hiking, towns, hotels, restaurants, and stores who really don't want you there). "That will shoot adrenaline into your souls!" (That will keep you on trail as an AT thru-hiker and as a follower of Jesus on the trail of life.)

The Way

Most people are surprised to find that the term "Christian" is mentioned only three times in the entire Bible. Acts 11 states that the disciples were first called Christians at Antioch. It is believed the term was used derogatorily when referring to the "Christ Ones." The second use of the term is found in Acts 26 where King Agrippa mockingly says to Paul, who was on trial before him, "Do you think that in such a short time you can persuade me to be a Christian?" (NIV). Then Peter writes in 1 Peter 4: "Yet if anyone suffers as a Christian, let him not be ashamed, but let him glorify God in that name."

Although Peter does state that believers should not be ashamed of the name *Christian*, we find that Christians referred to themselves by another term. Jesus had called Himself "The Way," and His followers called themselves followers of The Way. In Acts 9 Saul went to Damascus hoping to find those who belonged to The Way in order to bring them to Jerusalem to stand trial. Later in Acts 19 we find Saul, now a believer, going by the name Paul, living in Ephesus, and proclaiming the message he once so strongly opposed. Opponents of his message spoke evil of The Way, and a great disturbance erupted concerning The Way. In Acts 22 Paul states he used to persecute The Way, but he now worships God according to The Way. Lastly, Acts 24 states that Felix had a rather accurate knowledge of The Way.

What's the point? Remember that in the Bible the word "walk" is the most-used metaphor to describe life. I have found that thinking of life as a long-distance walk has been extremely helpful in trying to live life well, and it seems that the best way to understand and live the Christian faith is to realize it is a way of life by which followers of Jesus, The Way, strive to walk a particular path of life that Jesus lived and taught.

ANGELS IN FLIGHT—TRAIL MAGIC: PEOPLE WHO SHARE AT JUST THE RIGHT TIME

Fresh Ground

Fresh Ground

Trail Angels are people who come out to the trail to help meet hikers' needs in various ways, usually with food. It would take the remainder of the book to share all the wonderful Trail Angels we met, and I thank them all . . . but one Trail Angel stands out. He was a true Trail Angel as he warmed us up with hot food and drinks during the cold and snowy first couple months of the hike, and his North Carolina accent, continuous talk, and contagious laughter warmed us up as well.

Fresh Ground is a "southern boy" from North Carolina. He loves Jesus, and he loves hikers. He was planning to hike the trail in 2013, but he decided first to spend two days providing hot coffee, hot chocolate, and hot chicken soup at a road crossing in northeast Georgia at his own expense. He did have an unlabeled donation can off to the side with a slit in the lid and a paper sign near the table of food with the words of Jesus in Matthew 11:28: "Come unto me all you who are burdened and heavy laden, and I will give you rest" (NLT). He certainly did that for many weary hikers.

Fresh Ground's tent and table came to be known as Fresh Ground's Leapfrog Café. It earned the name "Leapfrog" because Fresh Ground kept moving north and leapfrogging the same hikers at various road crossings. He did so for the next two months and four states. His café, although wonderful in the beginning, became even better with each encounter. Through donations, he began to serve bacon and eggs, pancakes, donuts, coffee, hot chocolate, and juice for breakfast. Three times I caught him later in the day where he served salad, fresh fruit, sandwiches, hot dogs, hot soup, fried chicken, fried potatoes, and more. He also sent hikers back on the trail with doggie bags.

On his Facebook page he wrote, "What started out as a two day feed in GA, turned into a little over two-month feeding frenzy in four states. Donations from hikers and hiker families kept the cafe going... I look back and feel like we became family. Was such an honor to be trusted to provide for this year's hikers."

All along the trail I was moved by the generosity of those who love and desire to serve hikers. Fresh Ground knew hikers' needs and always provided a place to sit and rest while he tried to get us to eat another hot dog. It was evident to all who met him that Fresh Ground had gone through a shake down in life, was "traveling light," and had come to find rest and joy in life. I know if Fresh Ground were to add a few words to this post, he would say, as he did on the trail, "All thanks goes to Jesus; I'm just grateful to get to serve hikers."

He stands out in his love of and service for hikers and does so motivated by his love of and service for Jesus.

The Gift That Kept on Giving

Studying the Christmas story, I have been amazed at the distances traveled by the main characters referred to in the event. Those who traveled the farthest were the Magi or wise men. There isn't actually a number given as to how many there were. Three has been assumed because three gifts were given. We're also not told the distance they traveled but only that they came from the East. Many scholars believe they traveled by camel or horse nearly eight hundred miles from the ancient country of Persia to the little village of Bethlehem. By the time they got there, Joseph and Mary and Jesus were living in a home. It was a long journey over rough terrain.

Angels in Flight—Trail Magic: People Who Share at Just the Right Time

The Magi remind me of Trail Angels we met while hiking the AT. Many traveled several miles in order to help us in any way they could and to present us with the gifts of trail magic. In Vermont, Steve met Rash and me in the woods with a grill, hamburgers, hot dogs, chips, and drinks. In Maine, Grandma Sylvia drove an hour into the one-hundred-mile wilderness on a rutted logging road to surprise hikers with coffee and donuts from Dunkin' Donuts. Stickman drove well over two hundred miles to pick me up at Millinocket to assist me in getting home after reaching Mount Katahdin. He refused payment but instead presented me with an engraved hiking stick.

As it turned out, Joseph and Mary really needed the expensive gifts they were given because immediately after the Magi departed, they had to flee as fugitives nearly four hundred miles to Egypt to escape the clutches of the crazed King Herod. They most likely relied upon the trail magic from the Trail Angels to pay their travel expenses. The Magi returned home by another route, and no further mention is made of them. I am sure they never knew how crucial their gifts were to Joseph, Mary, and Jesus and that they would be recognized, written, and sung about two thousand years later. We should never underestimate the impact of even a small act of kindness.

Patch Hostel

Although I would stay in many excellent hostels along the trail, the Blueberry Patch Hiker Hostel near Hiawassee, Georgia, would prove to be special. The *Appalachian Trail Thru-Hikers' Companion* describes the hostel as a Christian ministry owned and operated by former thru-hiker Gary Poteat and his wife, Lennie.[5] From the time hikers arrive, the Poteats are there to serve each one, knowing their specific needs as only a thru-hiker could.

Gary memorizes each hiker's real and trail name. He kindly shows each hiker around the humble yet clean bunkhouse, which can accommodate up to ten hikers. Behind the bunkhouse is a restroom complete with a shower with great water pressure and very hot water. The couple provides towels, soap, and shampoo. Their hospitality includes laundry service, including loaner clothes to wear while everything is washed.

Gary gives hikers rides to Hiawassee, seven miles away, so they can resupply and eat at a restaurant. He shares his phone number for the return trip to the Blueberry Patch when the hikers are ready.

The couple serves a hearty family-style breakfast and then gives rides back to the trailhead. During my stay, nine hikers gathered around a large table to enjoy the thru-hiker-worthy meal prepared and served by Gary and Lennie. Before digging in, Gary asked us to join hands for prayer. Included in his prayer was the request that we all have a safe, blessed journey and that we would all come to a knowledge of Jesus Christ if that were not already true. An envelope was discreetly placed by each of our plates for donations if we felt led to contribute to the ministry of Blueberry Patch Hostel. Gary and Lennie do not charge for their services: it is all a gracious gift.

I don't know the religious background of those at the table that morning, but I do know that they were all deeply moved and not in the least bit offended by the envelopes or prayer. Gary and Lennie were excellent examples of loving servanthood and sensitivity to needs. They lovingly shared their faith in deeds and words without being pushy or offensive. One hiker later stated that it was enough to make him return to church. Another hiker, who plans to open his own restaurant in the future, said that the experience profoundly affected the type of atmosphere he hopes to have in his restaurant one day. He wants to reproduce the communal experience and have his customers feel as graciously served. He didn't mention whether he would operate on a donation basis, though!

Family, Food, and Friends

My friends Gordon and Judy live close to the Trail in Tennessee, and they housed and fed Sparks, Joe the Hiker, and me for several nights as we hiked through their area.

The great surprise was that their son Scott, his wife Kim, and five of their six children came over for supper. I performed their wedding nearly twenty-five years ago. It was a blessing to sit at the table with Scott and his family, his parents, Sparks, and Joe the Hiker. Our trail suppers were typically freeze-dried dinners gulped down in our sleeping bags while trying to stay warm. It made us realize how wonderful sharing a meal with family and friends can be.

The topic of food is prevalent in Scripture. Meals were a shared experience and were not rushed. In Revelation 3 Jesus says He desires to have supper with us. The word "supper" here refers to the long evening meal that was shared with family and friends. Gordon and Judy certainly lived out that Scripture as they served three weary hikers.

A Cup of Water

Nomad approached me in Erwin, Tennessee, and told me he felt called by God to get off the trail. Instead, he bought a van, filled it with food, and began showing up at road crossings to offer trail magic. He then gathered injured hikers to ride with him who helped serve other hikers while they healed up. He also transported hikers to various destinations, such as a doctor's office. He took Joe the Hiker to the airport to fly home and surprise his daughter by attending an awards ceremony. Nomad was serving this linear hiking community on the AT by offering a "cold cup of water in Jesus' name."

Hoosier and Roadrunner

Roadrunner Beep Beep

In the Smokies we had snow drifts over four feet deep to hike through. However, someone had pioneered the way and "broken trail" for us. I found out later it was a long, lanky hiker from Germany named Roadrunner. Not only was the path covered with snow but also the white blazes on the trees, which made finding them challenging.

When I came across Roadrunner later, I thanked him for going out before us. He said it was very difficult and that he was able to cover only around seven miles a day. He was genuinely moved that I would thank him. I also gave him two donuts I was carrying for a personal snack. He knew then that I was extremely grateful.

When I first met Roadrunner in the Smokies, it was a rough day for him. Sparks and I arrived at a shelter having caught the beginning of a storm. We experienced some rain, which then turned to sleet and hail. Roadrunner came in a few hours later drenched and shivering, having caught the full brunt of the storm. We told him to get in his sleeping bag and warm up while we made him hot food and coffee. He spoke little. I was fearful that he was going into hypothermia. However, early the next morning he thanked us and then hit the trail.

The book of Hebrews states that Jesus is the author and finisher of our faith. It is actually the picture of one going before and breaking trail for others to follow. Roadrunner was a picture of Jesus who went before us clearing out the obstacle of sin, which separated us from the Father, making salvation possible and showing us the path of life. He continues to do so as the finisher of our faith as well. Our faith journey continues as we daily trust Him to clear out obstacles and show us the right path.

The Iceman Cometh

Pennsylvania (Rocksylvania) could not have been accomplished without the help I received from a Mennonite Trail Angel named Iceman. Iceman lives over an hour from the trail near the Amish/ Mennonite community of Lancaster. After reading my journal entry about trying to catch up with friends, he spent three days driving to the trail and slack packing me in order to help me catch up with them. He even took me to his home one night and had me back to the trail at 6:30 the next morning. He was a true Trail Angel giving trail magic.

Pennsylvania may be where boots go to die, but it was full of Trail Angels who put a spring in our steps.

The Graymoor

One evening I arrived at a ball field on the grounds of The Graymoor Spiritual Life Center in Garrison, New York, run by a group of friars who allow hikers to camp there for free. It is less than a half-mile from the trail. They also provide port-a-johns, water, electricity, and a solar shower. The Graymoor Spiritual Life Center, noted for its hospitality, is a part of the Franciscan Order founded by Francis of Assisi in the 1200s.

Scripture has much to say about hospitality. Probably the best-known verse on the subject is found in Hebrews, which states that we ought to be hospitable, for in doing so, we may unknowingly host angels. If you had smelled me before the cold shower, you would know I am no angel, unless perhaps a fallen angel.

Angels in Flight—Trail Magic: People Who Share at Just the Right Time

Giving Through the Storm

While storms were brewing one night in Tennessee, Sparks, Mot, Punkin Pie, and I got off the trail and hitched a couple miles to Troutdale Baptist Church, which has a bunk house out back for hikers. Troutdale Baptist Church is very small but has a huge ministry to thru-hikers. It was actually the pastor's wife who picked us up. We slept indoors through the terrible storm.

In the morning we hiked just a few hours to a point where a longtime friend of mine picked Sparks and me up and took us to a hotel for the night. He also treated us to an all-you-can-eat buffet. Kevin arrived with a trunk full of trail magic, which we gave to around a dozen hikers we had been hiking with and who had tented through the storm. It was so much fun surprising them with grapes, oranges, apples, juice, and sandwiches. Jesus was right when He said, "It is more blessed to give than to receive."

TRAVELING WITH DELIGHT: ENJOYING THE JOURNEY

Walk Slowly (and Carry a Big Hiking Stick)

Memorial Day weekend I left Pennsylvania to return home so that I could conduct a friend's wedding. The bride's father told me that his barber gave him some advice for the wedding. He told him to walk very slowly down the aisle to the altar, and when he thinks he is going too slowly, he should slow down even more. The barber told my friend that he ought to relish the walk down and to walk slowly in order to take it all in.

I thought about that advice as I drove to Pennsylvania to begin the second half of the thru-hike: I should probably slow down and enjoy this journey more. I should savor it. I knew that too soon it would be over, and I would have only pictures and memories. I knew I didn't want to look back at this hike with regret; I wanted to enjoy each day.

Trail Names

On the trail, people do not go by their real names but rather by a trail name they have been given or chosen while hiking the trail. This new name reflects their new identity as a thru-hiker. It is frowned upon to ask someone his or her real name or profession off trail. In Scripture we find that God would often change a person's name to reflect the new identity. One example in the Old Testament would be Jacob whose name was changed to Israel, and in the New Testament we have Simon whose name was changed to Peter. Both men over time lived lives that reflected the character depicted in their new names. The book of Revelation chapter two states that God has given His children new names. He wants us to live out our new identities as His children. It is worth reflecting upon what new names God might have given us and if we are living out that new identity.

White Rocks

Stone Markers

When I made it to Damascus, Virginia, after completing the Georgia, North Carolina, and Tennessee sections of the trail, I knew I had completed around twenty percent of the AT with only around 1,700 miles to go. I looked at the trail in segments to see how far it was to the next trail town where we could resupply, eat real food, take a shower, and sleep indoors for a night. These segments were usually around sixty to seventy-five miles apart. At that point, reaching Mt. Katahdin at the end of the journey was too much to consider.

In 2007 when I hiked Vermont, New Hampshire, and Maine, I arrived at White Rocks on July 4th in 2007 and in 2013. This was a very special place for me. Throughout history and in many cultures, people have set up stones to commemorate the fact that their god or gods either met them or brought them safely to that point in their journey. All over Israel there are such locations where large stones have been set up. In Genesis 29, Jacob sets up and anoints a stone he used as a pillow and names it Bethel, which means "House of God." He does so because God met him there, spoke to him, and made promises to him. Many years later Jacob returned to the same spot and named it El Bethel, which means "House of the Mighty One." God had kept His promises to Jacob, and he now knew God as the Mighty God who keeps His promises, does more for us than we ever dreamed, and watches over us. Similarly, God told Samuel to set up a large stone in the place where a great victory over the Philistines had occurred. Samuel named the stone Ebenezer, meaning "stone of remembrance or help," because the Lord delivered them there from the Philistines.

Likewise, we ought to have memorials in our lives to commemorate milestones in our spiritual journeys.

In 2007 upon arriving at White Rocks, I remember thanking God that He had brought me safely not only to that point on the journey but also the journey of life. In 2013 I thanked Him for bringing me not just around one hundred miles but around 1,700. More than that, God also brought me safely to a new chapter of life as a retired minister and given me health and abundant blessings. I believe I know Him even better this time as El Bethel, the Mighty One.

Hotel? Or Prison?

In Kent, Connecticut, I met a friend, ate restaurant food, and slept in a real bed. It was wonderful! I re-entered the mosquito-infested trail getting water out of a stream and eating Ramen noodles and Spam for supper, which reminded me of some statements C.S. Lewis wrote about life. He said that half the people think life is like staying in a luxury hotel, and the other half think it is more like a prison. The first group is very disappointed, and the other half is pleasantly surprised. He also stated that God gives us some refreshing inns along the journey of life but would encourage us not to confuse them with home.[6]

I was grateful for the brief refreshing break I had from the trail but knew that most of the journey would be spent in the woods with the mosquitoes. Even that was not a prison.

~~Don't~~ DO Look Down

When hiking, ninety-nine percent of the time is spent looking at the ground. If I looked around while hiking, I would fall within a few steps. Periodically I would come to a vista where I could stop to take in the view. At one vista in New Hampshire, I stopped and spent around fifteen minutes talking with three young south bounders. They shared stories of the trail in Maine, and I shared what was ahead for them. When I was ready to leave, they said I was the first north bounder who had stopped and spoken with them for more than a few seconds. They said north bounders seemed to be tired of the trail and just wanted to get it over with, that they were putting in big miles to get to Katahdin.

Some hikers were under pressure to complete the trail because of obligations that fall. I was not under that kind of pressure. Instead, I desired to enjoy the remainder of the hike. I knew I would look back at it with enjoyment, but I wanted to enjoy the trail every day.

The Gear Between the Ears

At home one morning I received an email from an outfitter company advertising their "Semi-Annual Upgrade Your Gear Sale." *Gear:* it always grabs a thru-hiker's attention. Before the hike, a lot of study goes into what gear to purchase—a lot of money, too! A good rule to follow is the lighter, the more expensive. During the early stages of the hike, there were many discussions and comparisons about gear, questions like, "Are you satisfied with it? How much does it weigh, and how much did it cost?" However, with time, those conversations seemed to die out. We came to realize that although gear is important, even more important is the "gear between the ears": attitude.

After reading the advertisement, I read the letter of Philippians. Paul wrote it as a prisoner under house arrest in Rome. However, even in that difficult situation, he had a very positive attitude. The words *thankfulness*, *joy*, and *rejoicing* appear over and over again. Paul repeats the word *rejoice* so many times that he states, "To write the same things to you [rejoice] is no trouble to me . . . " (3:1). Then in 4:4 he writes, "Rejoice in the Lord always; again I will say, Rejoice."

How could he maintain such a positive attitude in such a situation? I believe one answer is found at the conclusion of the letter where he writes, "All the saints greet you, especially those of Caesar's household" (4:22). Paul was accomplishing his goal of sharing the gospel of Jesus Christ even while in prison. Even the imperial guard assigned to guard him was coming to faith (1:12).

So as a thru-hiker on the trail and on the trail of life, we need to remember that it is the "gear between the ears" that matters more: maintaining a positive attitude in any situation and pursuing goals consistently.

White Rocks Bridge

The Biggest Bridge

In White Rocks, Vermont, the trail passes through an area with white rocks scattered indiscriminately upon the ground. It is customary for hikers to pick up a rock and place it upon others, creating a cairn to mark the trail where white blazes cannot be seen. However, hikers have begun building other interesting rock formations here as well. One such structure in particular caught my eye. It forms a bridge between two large boulders. A rock slab spans the gulf between the two, and several small rocks are balanced on top of the slab.

To me this bridge symbolizes what the Bible calls the Gospel, i.e., the Good News of how to have a relationship with God. The left boulder represents all humanity and the right boulder, God. The rock slab bridging the gulf between the two represents Jesus Christ. Paul wrote in I Timothy 2:5-6a, "For there is one God and one mediator [bridge] between God and mankind, the man Christ Jesus, who gave himself as a ransom for all people."

I placed my rock on top of the long slab spanning the gulf between God and men. On the AT I attempted to live and share my faith in such a way that I would play at least a small part in causing fellow hikers to desire a relationship with God and consider the gospel of Jesus Christ.

Paul goes on to write that Jesus "gave himself as a ransom [the payment paid to set one free] for all people" (NIV). "All people" would include all the hikers I grew to know, respect, and love on the AT, and these hikers could be a second symbol for the rocky bridge. As I have stated before, there is a great diversity of people on the AT whose common path and destination of the trail bring them together in a unique way. The same is true with those who have a relationship with God through his Son Jesus. There is a common path and destination.

They say a picture is worth a thousand words. To me, this ordinary white rock formation in the Green Mountains of Vermont is worth a million words.

Forgotten Pain

Jesus said in John 16:21, "A woman giving birth to a child has pain because her time has come; but when her baby is born she forgets the anguish because of her joy that a child is born into the world" (NIV). Thru-hikers, like the new mother, tend to forget the pain we went through on our way to Katahdin as we reminisce about the journey. I was recently looking at a picture of a beautiful green swampy area on the trail. The AT traverses through the swamp for hundreds of yards on bog boards. While enjoying the beautiful scene, I suddenly remembered how slippery the boards were, how I slipped into the swamp, and came up soaked and swarmed by mosquitoes. It all seems quite hilarious now. I am glad we tend to forget the pain of the journey and focus instead upon the joy afterward. I wish I enjoyed it more at the moment it was happening. Several times I remember thinking that if I could just disassociate from the pain I was feeling, this would be the most awesome experience. Ecclesiastes 3:12-13 says, "I perceived that there is nothing better for them than to be joyful and to do good as long as they live; also that everyone should eat and drink and take pleasure in all his toil—this is God's gift to man."

Orthodox rabbis teach that we humans will have to answer to God if we don't enjoy all the good gifts He has given us for our journey here on earth. An expression often heard on the trail is "enjoy the journey." That is a good saying to live by on the trail of life, too. After all, we don't want to answer to God for not enjoying life, do we?

TRAVELING WITH THE END IN SIGHT: STAYING COMMITTED DESPITE THE DIFFICULTY

Hobos and Turtles

In New Jersey I saw a turtle crawling down the trail, which got me thinking that even a turtle could complete the trail if it were committed. I looked up some facts on box turtles:

Average distance:	.2 miles per day
Average lifespan:	40 years
Miles per year:	53
Miles walked in a lifetime:	2,120 (average)
Distance of Appalachian trail:	2,185 (close!)

The next morning I started hiking at 5:30 A.M. and had made only ten miles at 11 A.M. It was very cold, windy, and rainy. At times the trail was a foot deep in water, and the rocky balds were slick. Nomad was in the area, so he picked me up and took me to REI, where I bought new boots and new pants that fit my scrawny body.

Recently a friend jokingly called me a hobo. I think there is some truth in the statement. Both thru-hikers and hobos live off what they carry on their backs. They have to trust that their basic needs will be met. It reminds me of that turtle. In Hebrews chapter 11 the heroes and heroines of the faith lived like hobos and turtles. Living like this is actually quite freeing and builds faith. Jesus had quite a bit to say about commitment, too, such as counting the cost of being a follower of His on the path of righteousness.

Yes, I Am

After I entered New York, people often asked if I was a thru-hiker. They congratulated me and almost stood in awe. This surprised me because I have always been told that people in the East are somewhat cool and aloof, but I found the opposite to be true. I felt like a seasoned hiker.

Earlier when asked if I were a thru-hiker, I would answer that that was my intent; however, around this time I began to say, "Yes, I am." I realized I could be off the trail at any minute with an injury. Still, I thought I could truthfully say yes because it defined who I am. Similarly, after years of following Jesus, Christians should have the confidence to state, "Yes, I am a follower of Jesus on the path of righteousness, and I am committed to finishing well."

An Independence Day Reunion

When I arrived in Manchester Center, Vermont, excitement was in the air. Hikers I had not seen in months had hiked hard to get into town by the Fourth of July. It was like a family reunion. There were smiles, high fives, and hugs all around when we saw familiar faces and realized we were still on trail. There was sadness in hearing of fellow hikers who were no longer able to hike for various reasons. One hiker on this, his third attempt, made it into Massachusetts and then could not continue due to persistent foot problems.

It must have been similar for Paul, Timothy, Titus, Silas, Barnabas, and others who at times met and rejoiced that they were still on trail. I am also sure there was dejection upon hearing of those who no longer were following Jesus. For several years Demas was a companion of the Apostle Paul's. Paul referred to him as a faithful servant and fellow soldier. However, years later he wrote to Timothy and asked him to come quickly to give him aid because Demas had forsaken him, having fallen "in love with this present world" (II Timothy 4:10).

In the early stages of the hike, there were those who left the trail because they missed the comforts of the world. That was not true of the majority of those who quit the hike later. It was usually due to injuries or sickness. It was sobering to realize that each of us was only one wrong step away from going home. It was a humbling walk.

The ~~Song~~ Trail That Never Ends

Late in the hike I read a shelter journal entry written by Wild Rain. Her entry played off the children's song "The Song that Never Ends" from the CD *Lamb Chop's Sing-Along, Play-Along*.[7] She wrote, "This is the trail that doesn't end. Yes, it goes on and on, my friends. Some people started hiking it not knowing what it was, and they'll continue hiking it forever, just because."

I assume she meant it humorously, but then again, maybe she was having a tough day. The songs lyrics and tone are repeated over and over without purpose or resolution and were typically sung by children when doing something repetitive and boring. I think every thru-hiker would agree that there are days on the trail that seem repetitive and at times boring. Many hikers find Virginia to be so. The trail in Virginia is over five hundred miles long and is known as the "green tunnel" with "puds," i.e. pointless ups and downs. Many hikers drop out in Virginia. I have found that the only thing to do at such times is to take the next step forward knowing that it brings me that much closer to my goal. But what if it were true that the trail had no end? Then why take another step? Life off trail can seem repetitive and boring at times as well. How do we "stay on trail" at such times? We must believe that there really is an end and that each step brings us closer to a glorious goal.

Wild Rain hiked with a favorite verse that she paraphrased and attached to her pack, which read, "Those who trust in the Lord shall possess the land and inherit his holy mountain" (Isaiah 57:13). That truth inspired her all the way to Mount Katahdin. It will also get her to other mountain tops in life and a glorious inheritance after her life's journey.

Encouragement as High as a Mountain

The Whites of New Hampshire were awesome, majestic, beautiful, difficult, and dangerous. The weather could change in a moment, drenching me in cold rain that penetrated my bones and blowing me about in high winds that could almost send me flying over a cliff. Climbing up and over Mount Madison proved

Wild Rain

to be one of my toughest days. The trail there is a field of huge jagged boulders. Hiking poles are useless as they get stuck in deep crevices between boulders. Therefore, I was able to average only around one mile per hour. I was thanking God that I wasn't dealing with mud, bugs, roots, ticks, high winds, or cold rain. I consoled myself by remembering that each step, though slow and tedious, was a step closer to Katahdin. However, I began questioning whether I had "what it takes" to be a thru-hiker. After all, I still had over three hundred tough miles ahead of me.

Right when I needed it most, I received some very encouraging words. A day-hiker passed me and asked where I was going. I said Maine. He said, "I know that; you have the look. I mean, where are you going *today*?" I said Osgood Tent-site and went on. However, his words encouraged and stayed with me, even if "the look" meant skinny, smelly, dirty, disheveled, hairy, and hungry.

When I finally arrived at Osgood Tent-site, I was greeted by Shutterbug, a thru-hiker I had not seen since Tennessee. When she saw me, she said, "Hey, Hoosier, I knew you would still be on trail." What an encouragement! She believed I had what it took to be a thru-hiker and said that to me on one of my most difficult days of the hike.

The word *encourage* appears over one hundred times in the New Testament. It means to come alongside of and speak to the need of the moment so as to strengthen, inspire, embolden, console, comfort, and give confidence. The two people who encouraged me that day probably had no idea how much I needed their words. Proverbs 18:21 states, "Words kill, words give life; they're either poison or fruit" (The Message). Their words were life-giving words and bore the fruit of continuing on toward Katahdin.

Amazing Grace

Fall in Maine... the air was cool and crisp, and the skies were sunny and blue. As I crossed over the amazing Bigelow Mountain range, which is also the two-thousand-mile mark, I reviewed this journey that began March 2. As I did so, one of the verses to "Amazing Grace" came to mind. The words express well my thoughts upon reaching this milestone. "Through many dangers, toils, and snares I have already come. 'Tis grace hath brought me safe thus far, and grace will lead me home"[8] (to Mount Katahdin).

The End Is in Sight

One hundred thirty-seven trail miles away, I saw Mount Katahdin. Hebrews 11 speaks of the heroes and heroines of the faith who believed in the promises of God even when they had not yet seen them fulfilled. The passage says they admitted that they were pilgrims on the earth and continued walking by faith until faith became sight.

Our spiritual life is much like this trail. We walk through many difficulties in life with seemingly no end in sight. However, there really is an end, and a God, a Savior, and Heaven. Just wait and see.

Monson, Maine

Monson, Maine, is a very small, struggling, but blessed town located on a logging truck route in northern Maine right before the final Hundred-Mile Wilderness. Many of the small storefronts are closed, and several buildings are in bad shape. However, I like it. Monson is located on the shore of Lake Hebron. In Scripture, Hebron is the city that Caleb captured from the Canaanites when he was eighty-five years old. It was later established as a city of refuge in Israel. Those who committed unintentional crimes could flee there for protection and find safety from retaliation. The word *Hebron* means alliance or companion. Monson is a hiker-friendly town and also the home to the AIIA Institute, an excellent source for answers to biblical questions.

On the shore of Lake Hebron is the Lake Shore House, an extremely hiker-friendly hostel/hotel with a wonderful restaurant. Rebekah, the owner, is a gracious servant to hikers. So in reality, Monson is blessed and a wonderful trail town to zero in. It is also the last town before Katahdin.

THE JOY OF COMPLETION AND TRANSITION TO LIFE OFF-TRAIL

It Is Finished

Tetelestai

Punkin Pie joined me with the intent of hiking the final 115 miles of the AT. However, after only three days he needed to return home. It was great reuniting and hiking with him. After his departure, I hiked alone through the Hundred-Mile Wilderness for the final four days. I can truly say, though, that I was not alone. God has never been more real to me than during those last few days. I had a lot of time to reflect.

One thing I thought about was the pose I wanted to depict at the Katahdin sign. Most I have seen are a depiction of victory with arms stretched out in triumph. I am not in any way saying that is wrong, but for me it would not be expressing my true thoughts of the moment.

I wanted my pose to give God the glory. Therefore, in my summit photos I stretched one hand to the heavens with a finger pointing to God. I wanted to express gratitude to Him for His presence, protection, and provision throughout every mile of the journey. It truly is only by His grace that I arrived at that sign. My other arm is reaching out, and a finger is pointing to supporters whom God used as His instruments to make the completion of the journey possible. I am pointing to those who supported me financially, through prayers, words of encouragement, help with technology (posting a journal entry), and on the journal. I am pointing to all the Trail Angels who gave trail magic, food, a bed for the night, and a hitch for a tired, hungry, dirty, stinky hiker who needed to get to a trail town to resupply. I am pointing to fellow hikers who shared in the same daily struggle to put in our miles going north. I have never been a part of such an eclectic group of people. My fellow hikers were my favorite part of the journey. While reflecting upon all of them, I got all choked up and cried, which is uncommon for me. I will never forget all of them, although I don't know most of their real names. The journey was hard and long, but they made it fun.

I thought of my wife Jan, who for over twenty years has known of my dream to one day hike the entire AT in one calendar year, and thus earn the title thru-hiker. Over the years she has supported me in my one- or two-week hikes and even a two-month hike in 2007. This hike took me half a year, and she knows what the title thru-hiker means to me.

Bruised and Battered But Unbroken

As I have shared, statistics show that only around twenty percent of those who attempt a thru-hike will have a picture of themselves at Springer Mountain and on Mount Katahdin. Ecclesiastes 7:8 states, "Better is the end of a thing than its beginning." Israel's wise king Solomon also observed and wrote in Ecclesiastes 9:11 that "the race is not always to the swift, nor the battle to the strong, nor bread to the wise, nor riches to the intelligent, nor favor to those with knowledge, but time and chance happen to them all."

I am humbled by the fact that I have a picture of myself at Springer and Katahdin. I could list many hikers who were stronger, swifter, smarter, and more skilled than I who did not complete the journey. Time and chance occurred, a slippery rock, bad knees, shin splints, giardia, Lyme disease: a multitude of things can take a hiker "off trail." Every day I realized that just one misstep out of an estimated five million could have ended the journey for me as well. I was extremely careful the last few days as I could see Katahdin in the distance. Northern Maine's terrain is a slippery jumble of rocks, roots, and mud. I fell everyday. However, though bruised and battered, nothing was broken, and I was able to go on, which reminds me of another verse written by Solomon from the book of Proverbs: "for the righteous man may fall seven times and rises again" (24:16). By God's grace I was able to get back up.

Paling in Comparison

My wife Jan and I had the privilege of hearing Jennifer Pharr Davis speak. She holds the record for the fastest assisted thru-hike on the AT. She has hiked it three times, as well as the PCT and many other trails. She shared about the difficulties she went through in accomplishing the record. She suffered much: shin splints, diarrhea, near hypothermia, and extreme body aches and pains. Yet she exuded a deep love for hiking and the AT. Her love for the trail and hiking was what she focused on, and I think all those in attendance were inspired to leave and take a hike.

The Apostle Paul knew pain and difficulty, too. He was often beaten and stoned, as II Corinthians 11 testifies. Yet he states in Romans 8 that he does not consider his present sufferings worth comparing to the glory that is coming. Earlier in II Corinthians 4 he writes that our light and momentary afflictions are preparation for an eternal weight of glory beyond all comparison. So my take-away is this: any sufferings thru-hikers go through to reach Katahdin will pale in significance with the joy of reaching that sign. Also, difficulties we go through on our spiritual journey will seem like nothing when we finish that trail.

God Looks at My Heart

When I first went off trail, it certainly seemed strange driving a car and going so fast. I noticed that others at the turnpike plazas found me a bit strange, too. In trail towns, thru-hikers are treated with respect even though we are quite grungy. In one trail town, a shuttle driver greeted hikers by jokingly stating, "You stink, and you are ugly. I don't care what your name is—real or trail name—because I will never see you again. Where you from?" He provided free shuttles from the trail to town and would not accept money. He actually liked hikers. It reminded me of the statement in the Bible: "Man looks on the outward appearance, but the LORD looks on the heart" (1 Samuel 16:7).

I did, however, clean up when I got home.

When the World Says Sick, God Says Healthy

Although there are many legends as to where the word *Hoosier* originated, from my study it seems most likely that it originated in England and refers to a person who is adept at living in the woods. Indiana was originally all woods with several Indian tribes living there. I live on Miami Road, an old winding ridge Indian trail named after the Miami Indians.

I have found it is more difficult to live well at home than in the woods. We can't just live in the woods. For instance, upon arriving home, I had to deal with a mountain of paper work dealing with various insurances, bank statements, medical bills, etc. I hate climbing that mountain. Give me a literal four-thousand footer instead.

Just before getting off trail for a short break, I was hiking with a section hiker who is a male nurse. When departing, I said,

"Well, back to the real world, huh." He replied, "That is not the real world. The world was never meant to be like it is. The world is sick!" I laughed and agreed and then had several miles of hiking alone to reflect upon his statement. The world *is* sick. Why do we try to fit into a sick world? Romans 12:2 states, "Do not be conformed to this world, but be transformed by the renewal of your mind..." On the trail we have time to think about how the world squeezes us into its mold and how before long, we fit in. I pray I am transformed to such a degree that I am healthy and do not fit into this sick world.

Pastor Hoosier

When I got off trail in Pennsylvania to perform a friend's wedding, I entered the church where I pastored for 26.2 years. Several people asked if I missed it. I do miss the people, but I do not miss being Pastor Clapper. I had a wonderful marathon pastorate there, but I am now Hoosier. My new sanctuary is the woods, and my new congregation is an eclectic group of dirty, smelly, hairy, hungry hikers, and I am one of them. I really like them, and I really like being Hoosier. Hoosier is still about the same person he was as a pastor, trying to be as much like Jesus as he can and serving others.

simplify

The Long Trail Inn at Killington, Vermont, has a very plain plaque on the wall that says, "Simplify." When I saw it, I was struck by the fact that life on the trail is simple, and I like life that way. Since returning home, I have come to realize that except for the physical aspect of the hike, life is actually much easier on the

The Joy of Completion and Transition to Life Off-Trail

trail than off. People have asked what reentry has been like for me. I must admit that I do prefer porcelain instead of a splintered wood privy seat and a soft feather pillow rather than my stinky clothes in a stuff sack serving as a pillow.

However, much of trail life I prefer over life off trail. Thru-hikers I have talked to voice the same desire to simplify life upon their return home, but like me find it difficult to do so. I have found the following quote from the writings of the Apostle Paul to be helpful: "Take your everyday, ordinary life—your sleeping, eating, going-to-work, and walking-around life—and place it before God . . . Don't become so well-adjusted to your culture that you fit into it without even thinking..." (Romans 12:1-2 The Message). It is worth thinking about.

Back to Rocksylvania

After completing the Trail, I attended the Appalachian Long Distance Hikers Association (ALDHA) gathering in Shippenburg, Pennsylvania. I really didn't want to return to Rocksylvania but attended because Punkin Pie and Mot said they were going to be there. I would return even to Pennsylvania to be with those guys. We all took our wives along and had a great time eating and laughing as we shared tales from the trail.

We, the thru-hikers class of 2013, received certificates of completion. Mine is made out to "Hoosier, formerly known as Craig Clapper." For the last half year I was known by the trail name Hoosier. I like who Hoosier was and became on the trail. I desire to live life off trail with the same character qualities Hoosier had on the trail. In many ways I feel that Craig Clapper died on the trail and the thru-hiker Hoosier was born and grew.

The Bible describes salvation as being "born again" and is also full of stories of people being renamed and becoming new people in character living up to the meaning of their new name. A letter of congratulations from ALDHA ends with the statement, "What you have accomplished is amazing. Don't forget what you have learned, and live your life as you hiked the trail." I plan and hope to do so and one day hear Jesus say, "Well done, thou good and faithful servant, enter ye into the joys of heaven."

Go Outside

I miss the trail ... not so much the hiking but rather living outdoors. I feel claustrophobic indoors. I firmly believe we humans were meant to spend much more time outside than we do. It puzzles me how much attention is given to the weather on the local news when people spend so little time out in it.

I read and reflected upon Psalm 19 written by the shepherd David. He spent much of his life living outdoors, first as a shepherd, then as a soldier, and later as a fugitive on the run. He states that day and night the heavens are declaring God's glory through his handiwork. Living under the sun, moon, and stars spoke volumes to him about God. Later he became the King of Israel and lived in a palace. I wonder if he wrote this Psalm while living outdoors or in the palace longing to be back out there like I do.

I miss the "voice" of nature. Having a roof over my head seems to hide the glory of God and muffles what is being declared by his handiwork. I recently had a friend share with me that she and a friend had watched a fantastic Fourth of July fireworks display. Later on a warm summer night, they were talking about the fireworks display while observing thousands of lightning bugs hovering over and lighting up a bean field. One looked at the other and said, "God wins!"

A few nights ago Samson and I slept out on a crystal-clear moonlit night under the stars in the desolate beauty of the Badlands of South Dakota. We saw the glory of God and heard His voice. The next night we slept in a very nice hotel that was decorated with nature scenes. God won again!

Why don't you go outside and read this section of Psalm 19 that I find so meaningful? That will make it even better. "The heavens declare the glory of God, and the sky above proclaims his handiwork. Day to day pours out speech, and night to night reveals knowledge. There is no speech, nor are there words, whose voice is not heard. Their voice goes out through all the earth, and their words to the end of the world. In them he has set a tent for the sun..." (verses 1-4).

Paul in Pennsylvania

I think Pennsylvania was my toughest state. I had heard about the rock fields that caused hikers to rename it Rocksylvania, Sprainsylvania, and Painsylvania. It's not that the rocks are huge; they aren't. It's not that the state is particularly steep; it isn't. It's just that much of the trail in Pennsylvania goes through miles of small, jagged, and loose rocks without a soft spot to step on. Instead, the day was spent walking on terrain that tore at my boots, cut my ankles, and bruised the bottoms of my feet. It also drained me emotionally since each step needed to be planned. I had to concentrate on foot placement.

Since returning to life off trail, I have found that life offers some of the same terrain Pennsylvania does—there are so many details that demand attention and concentration that it's a pain and wears me out. It also seems I never get around to what's most important. Thinking about this reminded me of the last words of Paul to Timothy found in II Timothy. Paul was an outdoorsman. He wrote that he was "constantly on the move." There are over thirteen thousand miles of his journeys recorded in his writings, much of them on foot over difficult terrain. At the end of his life, he is in prison awaiting a martyr's death. I assume being chained up in a prison is hard on a man who spent much of his life outdoors traveling by foot. However, he does have time to reflect and write while in prison. He speaks of his upcoming death as the end of his life's journey and seems to be looking forward to the finish. However, after waxing eloquently about his upcoming death, his tone abruptly changes. He has details to handle before death comes. He tells Timothy to come soon, before winter, and "when you come, bring the cloak I left with Carpus at Troas, also the books, and above all the parchments" (4:13). Even Paul is not exempt from having to deal with the mundane details of life. It seems he forgot his cloak and needs Timothy to bring it, his books, and parchments. Time is of the essence as well. "Do your best to come before winter" (4:21a).

Just as every thru-hiker must go through the rock fields of Pennsylvania to make it to Katahdin, we, too, must walk through the seemingly mundane and endless details of life to accomplish our goals. It is part of the journey. Embrace it, and remember that each step—no matter how tedious, boring, or painful—is a step toward accomplishing the goal.

The Joy of Completion and Transition to Life Off-Trail

Finally . . .

Statistics for the thru-hiking class of 2013 were published by the Appalachian Trail Conservatory. Although a record number of hikers began a thru-hike, only around fifteen percent completed the journey. Record-breaking snow and cold in March, continuous rain throughout the spring and summer, and a norovirus outbreak contributed to a lower-than-usual completion rate.

Another statistic that interested me was that of the little over fourteen thousand hikers who have completed a thru-hike, fewer than four percent have been over sixty years old. I turned sixty-three while on the trail and am greatly humbled that I completed the journey. Truly it was the grace of God that got me to Katahdin. Samson, my friend and fellow thru-hiker, claims he was the clumsiest hiker on the trail this year, but I think I was. Although I didn't keep count, I believe I fell every day and multiple times on some days. The AT traverses fourteen states; I think I have a scar from each state. Often, I would get back up after a fall and thank God that although bruised, battered, and bleeding, I was able to continue.

David wrote Psalm 18:33 while a fugitive on the run from King Saul in the rugged Judean Mountains. I have had the privilege of hiking that same area and have often seen ibex (deer) scaling the rugged cliffs. It is amazing how agile and sure footed they are. David, too, was able to scale those cliffs to escape Saul and his armies. This caused David to write, "He made my feet like the feet of a deer and set me secure on the heights." David was literally in the mountains and needed God's strength and agility to scale the rugged cliffs in order to escape from Saul. Later, Habakkuk, speaking of the difficult times he and the nation of

Israel were going through, wrote in Habakkuk 3:17-19, "Though the fig tree should not blossom, nor fruit be on the vines, the produce of the olive fail and the fields yield no food, the flock be cut off from the fold and there be no herd in the stalls, yet I will rejoice in the LORD; I will take joy in the God of my salvation. GOD, The Lord, is my strength; he makes my feet like the deer's; he makes me tread on my high places." Like the trail, life at times is very difficult. We need the "feet of a deer" in order to climb up and over the dangerous terrain. With God's strength and grace we can "walk on the high places" and complete life's journey with scars but unbroken.

BIBLIOGRAPHY

1. "The Appalachian Trail." *Planetanimals.* http://planetanimals.com/logue/atmap.html.
2. Carroll, Lewis. *Alice in Wonderland.* Scituate, MA: Digital Scanning Inc., 2007.
3. Yancey, Philip. *Disappointment With God: Three Questions No One Asks Aloud.* Grand Rapids: Zondervan Publishing House, 1988.
4. Appalachian Long Distance Hikers Association. *Appalachian Trail Thru-Hikers' Companion – 2011.* Harpers Ferry, WV: Appalachian Trail Conservancy, 2011.
5. Ibid.
6. Lewis, C.S. *The Problem of Pain.* New York: HarperCollins, 2002.
7. Martin, Norman. "The Song That Never Ends." *Lamb Chop's Sing-Along, Play-Along.* A&M Records, 1988. CD.
8. Newton, John. "Amazing Grace." 1779.

Craig (Hoosier) loves to travel and speak on *Legging It*. You can contact him at hikingclapper@gmail.com and get more information on his seminars at https://vimeo.com/channels/craigclapper .

CPSIA information can be obtained
at www.ICGtesting.com
Printed in the USA
BVOW08s0718260317
479466BV00001B/231/P